D0921979

SET FREE

How to break spiritual bonds

SET FREE

How to break spiritual bonds

by John Aston

LIVING BOOKS FOR ALL

Copyright © 1990 by Christian Literature Crusade

ALL RIGHTS RESERVED

Scripture quotations marked NIV are from the Holy Bible, New International Version, Copyright © 1973, 1978, 1984, International Bible Society. All other Scripture quotations are from the Good News Bible, © 1976, British & Foreign Bible Society, London.

ISBN: 962-7329-02-9

LIVING BOOKS FOR ALL
P.O. BOX 98425 (TST)
KOWLOON, HONG KONG

FOREWORD

"I wrote about all that Jesus began to do and to teach until the day he was taken up to heaven, after giving instructions through the Holy Spirit to the apostles he had chosen." Acts 1:1,2 (NIV)

This is essentially a book for those with a need. It contains vital information for those who need to know how others can be set free or who need to be set free themselves. It does not contain theological theory, but only that which John Aston has seen Jesus do, supported with biblical texts and containing instructions about how we may also do this vital work of setting people free through the Holy Spirit.

I first came to know John Aston nearly ten years ago through correspondence. At that time I was unconvinced and uncertain about demonic influences in the lives of Christians but had been faced many times with phenomena which I could not explain. John's letters about his own experiences and the way in which he prayed interested me. Some of what he shared with me is contained in this book. Since then he has taught much of this material among us here in Hong Kong. I have been enormously impressed with his teaching but more impressed by the results. Person after person who had dark areas, bondages, and unexplainable hindrances in their Christian lives have been set free to serve Jesus Christ and remain free to this day. I pray that in reading this material, the Holy Spirit would give your eyes and heart understanding, that He would add wisdom and power to you as you seek to effect this teaching in setting many free from the devil's work, in Jesus' name.

Jackie Pullinger
Hong Kong
April 1990

to the members of the

BIRMINGHAM CHINESE
CHRISTIAN FELLOWSHIP

many of whom are now in
Southeast Asia or scattered
around the world

CONTENTS

Acknowledgements

I would like to express my thanks to Jackie Pullinger who pushed me into writing the first draft of this book by inviting me to speak on this subject at the conference she held at Hang Fook Camp, Hong Kong in 1988. Even then, it would probably never have reached a readable form if Pat Lister had not been willing to type onto her word processor from my recorded dictation. At a later stage, Jean Mintoft improved the style and Mare Allison of CLC Hong Kong prepared it for publication.

I wish, even more, to express my thanks to many members, through many years, of the Birmingham Chinese Christian Fellowship. Without them, I should have had nothing to write about. Some of them appear in the book, but many others have contributed to it by teaching me about Chinese culture, by standing with me as we uncertainly tried things out together, and by praying with me and for me.

And there would have been no book but for Jesus, who defeated Satan by his death and resurrection, and gave authority to his people to use his name to overcome and destroy all the works of darkness.

INTRODUCTION

"Do you believe in evil spirits?" a young fellow asked me. "Yes, I do," I replied. The time was about 1972 and the place was the Birmingham Chinese Christian Fellowship, a Chinese church. But the young fellow was English. He had been attending our meetings for several weeks, perhaps because he thought we would be able to understand his problems better than the average English church would. And he had problems. Major problems. At that time, we did not have much teaching or experience but the Lord was giving us both, and that young fellow gave us a valuable opportunity to increase our experience as we gradually helped him to gain freedom from a great mass of evil influence which had come upon him from his family background.

About the same time, we encountered a Chinese family whose home had become almost uninhabitable because of the strange things that were going on in it. (Their story appears later in the book.) We also met several Chinese students whose spiritual growth was being hindered because of "things" in their possession which had a power that they had never taken seriously before.

Part of my working life has been spent teaching technology in a university. Some of the best courses we taught were described as "sandwich courses" because they consisted of alternate "slices" (6-month periods) of formal instruction in

5

the university and of practical work in the engineering industry. Sometimes I have found that God uses a similar pattern to teach us. I may have heard a talk or read a book which described how to deal with a certain spiritual problem. Soon after, I have encountered that very problem. Other times, I was faced with a problem, and then heard how someone had dealt with a similar situation. I hope this book will provide some instruction in biblical principles and will also illustrate how those principles can be worked out in church life. Do not be frightened if, after reading it, God gives you the opportunity to use what you have learned!

I was fortunate that, when I began to encounter the forces of evil directly at work in ordinary life, I did not have any mental or theological barriers to overcome. When I first invited Jesus into my life, as a student, I was mildly surprised, even slightly disappointed that nothing which I could call "supernatural" happened – no vision or deep inner experience. At that time I was quite prepared for some clear interaction between the spiritual and material worlds. In fact, I had to wait many years before I began to see this interaction, in such circumstances as healing the sick in direct response to prayer.

Because I took the Bible seriously when I read it, I accepted that the forces of evil, as well as the forces of God, interacted directly with the physical world, especially, but not only when Jesus was walking the earth. I was never taught that the powers of darkness had ceased their evil work in the world just as I was, fortunately, never taught that the Holy Spirit had stopped his good work in the world by means of his gifts to his people. So I continued to be open to the possibility of spiritual forces being at work in the world around me. I desired to see God's good work and mildly dreaded seeing the devil's evil work.

Many people exposed to Western theological and philosophical thinking have been less fortunate than I. They have, in effect, dropped the devil out of their world–view. This may be because they cannot reconcile his existence with the existence of an all-good, all-powerful God. It may be that they fear the people around them will think them stupid or ignorant if they acknowledge a real devil. It may be because, even though they fully acknowledge the existence of spiritual realities, good and evil, they think of them operating in a different world (perhaps a different dimension) from the world which we see and feel and which science describes for us. Or it may be because they have been persuaded that at the end of the New Testament period the direct work of the Holy Spirit through his gifts to his Church ceased, and by implication, the direct work of the devil ceased also. So, in the 19th century and through much of the 20th, most missionaries coming from the West to Asia and Africa had no thought of there being evil spirits at work in the world. Certainly, they had no teaching or training about dealing with them.

In contrast, most people in Asia and Africa have had frequent encounters with the forces of darkness, and to varying extents, realized the authority which Christ gave them to control those powers. Mrs. Howard Taylor, who worked with the China Inland Mission (now Overseas Missionary Fellowship) in Shan Xi province about 100 years ago, wrote a fascinating account of the life of Pastor Hsi, an outstanding Chinese Christian. Near the beginning she says, "It would never occur to a Chinese to question the existence of demons; he has too frequent proof of their power. We may regard such ideas as superstitious, and dismiss them without further thought. But facts remain: and some facts are startling as well as stubborn things." After Hsi became a Christian during a long struggle to give up opium, he became known as the "Conqueror of Demons." The book also describes his wife's experience:

> Always receptive and intelligent, she had grasped the truth with clearness. Her life had brightened and her heart enlarged, until it seemed as though she would become her husband's real fellow-worker and friend.

> Then, suddenly, all was changed; and her very nature seemed to change too. At first only moody and restless, she rapidly fell a prey to deep depression, alternating with painful excitement. Soon she could scarcely eat or sleep, and household duties were neglected. In spite of herself, and against her own will, she was tormented by constant sug-

gestions of evil, while a horror as of some dread nightmare seemed to possess her. She was not ill in body, and certainly not deranged in mind. But try as she might to control her thoughts and actions, she seemed under the sway of some evil power against which resistance was of no avail.

Especially when the time came for daily worship, she was thrown into paroxysms of ungovernable rage. This distressed and amazed her as much as her husband, and at first she sought to restrain the violent antipathy she did not wish to feel. But little by little her will ceased to exert any power. She seemed carried quite out of herself, and in the seizures, which became frequent, would use language more terrible than anything she could ever have heard in her life. Sometimes she would rush into the room, like one insane, and violently break up the proceedings, or would fall insensible on the floor, writhing in convulsions that resembled epilepsy.

Recognizing these and other symptoms only too well, the excited neighbors gathered round, crying, "Did we not say so from the beginning! It is a doctrine of devils, and now the evil spirits have come upon her. Certainly he is reaping his reward."

After her husband had prayed, Mrs. Hsi was completely changed. The villagers were amazed.

They had never before heard of anyone being cured of the effects of demons and many wanted to know more about Jesus. Incidentally, this story illustrates a common feature. The demons showed their presence more clearly the nearer Mrs. Hsi came to the Lord, perhaps because they had increasing fear that they were going to be cast out.

The episode that I have quoted was not an isolated experience. Later in the book Mrs. Taylor wrote,

> There is hardly a village on the Shan Xi plain without a spirit medium. Some calamity befalls a family – illness or disaster. Send for the medium at once. .... A striking feature in these cases is the apparent inability of the medium to shake off the control of the terrible power to which they have yielded. Unsought and contrary to their own desire, the over-mastering influence comes back, no matter how they may struggle against it.

Other missionaries of the same period were less ready to write about demonic manifestations. While preparing this introduction, I visited one of the best collections anywhere in the world of books about missionary work in China. I did not have time to check through all of them, but I looked in the index of a selection searching for words such as "demons," "deliverance," "exorcism," and "possession," with almost complete lack of success. In the introduction to the book about Pastor Hsi from which I have just quoted, D.E. Hoste, General Director of the CIM, considered it necessary to be cautious, even apologetic. He wrote,

Reference should be made here to a feature of this story which is likely to excite the wonder and even scepticism of many readers. I refer to the frequent allusions to demoniacal possession, and the casting out of evil spirits in answer to prayer, which occur throughout this book. . . . . Careful observation and study of the subject have led many to conclude that although, in lands where Christianity has long held sway, the special manifestations we are now considering are comparatively unknown; the conditions among the heathen being more akin to those prevailing when and where the Gospel was first propagated; it is not surprising that a corresponding energy of the powers of evil should be met with in missionary work to-day.

The tension between the skepticism of many Westerners, and the hard experience of most Asians, has been fully described by J.L. Nevius, an outstanding China missionary, in his book *Demon Possession.* Near the beginning he wrote, "I brought with me to China (i.e. in 1854) a strong conviction that a belief in demons, and communication with spiritual beings, belongs exclusively to a barbarous and superstitious age, and at present can exist only with mental weakness and lack of culture." But after several years in China, the agreement between the stories told by people in different localities, and the similarity to the accounts in the Scriptures, persuaded him to investigate. He decided to enquire of other missionaries and sent a letter to key men in many of the leading British and American missions then working in China. Most responded with detailed accounts of possession and deliverance. Nevius gives a total of forty-three case-histories, thirty-two of which are from China with the remainder from India, Japan and Europe. He analyzed the incidents carefully, and summarized with a list of features which are common to most or all of them. His final point is of great interest: "Many cases of 'demon-possession' have been cured by prayer to Christ, or in his name, some very readily, some with difficulty. So far as we have been able to discover, this method of cure has not failed in any case, however stubborn and long continued, in which it has been tried. And in no instance, so far as appears, has the malady returned, if the subject has become a Christian, and continued to lead a Christian life."

What happens when those who have been trained in the West and deny the reality of demonic effects meet those who have lived in Asia and are deeply aware of them? Simply this: the Asians stop talking about demons to those who don't believe. I have heard or read of this situation arising in China, Hong Kong, the Philippines, and different parts of Africa. Often, there is really very little difficulty with this solution. The church deals with the "big" matters and teaches about creation, the nature of God, salvation through faith in Jesus, and man's eternal destiny. More ordinary matters are taught about in the home, mainly by mother and grandmother. These are things like recovery from illness and how to be successful in business, marriage, pregnancy, and childbirth. If the church provides little guidance and less power to look after these needs, then people will go to those who offer them. This easy co-existence between two thought systems is well described by R.L. Henry in *Filipino Spirit World.* It is also similar to the mixed worship of the Lord and local gods or baalim by the Israelites in the Old Testament (further discussed later). If many church-goers have significant areas of their lives in which Jesus is *dis*honored because these areas are under the influence of enemy forces, then the church will not be strong.

Fortunately, there are many churches around the world where there is no such division, where the power of Jesus and of his Holy Spirit do penetrate into homely matters as well as into big issues. And these churches grow. It seems clear that healing and deliverance in the name of Jesus have been important factors in the growth of the church in China during the years in which that church has been largely cut off from the rest of the world. Indeed, this contrast in world-view and in attitude toward evil spirit powers and their interaction with the physical world may be related to the rapid church growth in many countries in Asia, Africa and Latin America. I have heard John Wimber say, at the end of a week of teaching and demonstration of *Signs and Wonders,* "Even if all I have done is to change your world-view, then my time has not been wasted." An inadequate (and incorrect) world-view which does not allow for direct interaction between the invisible and visible worlds greatly limits faith-expectancy.

I must add that when people first become aware of the reality of demonic activity, it is possible for them to become too excited and go too far. People may stress the work of demons so strongly that they fail to recognize human responsibility and ordinary sin. There is a danger in thinking that any difficulty or unhappiness can be dealt with by ordering a spirit to go – and that afterwards all will be well. We need to recognize that personal effort in self-control and in discipleship is essential, especially if there was no demon present!

In this book I have tried to use my training as a scientist to record my observations and experiences and to fit them into a biblical framework, a biblical world-view. Almost all the people I refer to are ethnic Chinese, most of whom live in Hong Kong, Malaysia and Singapore, although many of the events took place while they were studying in England. In most cases, perhaps all, I asked for and was given permission to use the episode for teaching purposes. I apologize if I have used any event against the wishes of the person concerned. In every case, the names of those being counseled have been changed, along with any identifying details. I have not thought it necessary to change the names of those working with me.

We will start by looking at some Biblical examples of conflict with and victory over the powers of darkness. Then we will go on to see some similar conflicts and victories in the contemporary world.

SPIRITUAL CONFLICT IN
THE BIBLE

Many passages in the Old Testament confront us with the fact that, not only does the Lord God of the Israelites truly exist and work, but also that numerous other spiritual beings exist and influence day-to-day events. The God of Israel revealed himself to his people and desired to draw them to himself and to teach them to live under his care and protection. Time and time again we see spiritual conflict when God's people failed to heed his warnings and turned to other gods.

We can find examples of this spiritual conflict near the beginning of the book of Exodus. God had called Abraham out of his own country and had led him to Canaan, which he had promised to give to Abraham's descendants. God had made a firm covenant with Abraham, in which he required Abraham and his descendants to worship him alone. Later, God repeated this covenant to Abraham's son Isaac and his grandson Jacob.

Years later there was a famine in Canaan and the whole family moved to Egypt. After several generations, they found themselves slaves, severely oppressed by their Egyptian taskmasters. They were so distressed that they cried out to their God for help. God called Moses to lead his people out of Egypt. Under God's direction, Moses precipitated a confrontation between Israel's God and the gods of the River Nile. This encounter is recorded in Exodus chapters 7 through 10. Let's look at Exodus 7:1 through 8:19 in some detail.

In the first encounter, Aaron threw his stick down in front of Pharaoh and his officials. It turned into a snake! The king called for his wise men and magicians, and each one of them, by their magic arts, was able to do exactly the same thing. (We can see equivalent phenomena today, e.g. in those who use evil forces to heal severe illnesses.) But the story did not end there; Aaron's snake swallowed up all the snakes which the magicians had produced!

The next stages in the conflict were a direct affront to the gods whom the Egyptians worshiped, the gods of the Nile (Osiris, Horus, etc.). God commanded Moses to stretch out his stick over the river, and the waters of the Nile turned to blood. Again, the King's magicians were able to imitate what God had done through Moses. If only they had been able to reverse what Moses had done, it would have been a real victory for Pharaoh and his magicians! When God told Aaron to stretch out his hand over the waters of Egypt, frogs came up and covered the land. The magicians were able to produce frogs, but they were not able to get rid of them. This left Pharaoh in the embarrassing position of having to ask Moses to rid the land of the frogs. Moses used the opportunity to point out to Pharaoh the superior power of the true God.

After this, God commanded Aaron to strike the ground with his staff. When he did this, the dust turned into swarms of gnats. It is interesting to note that it was the magicians who were the first to admit that God had done it. But even when the magicians told Pharaoh that this was the work of God and withdrew from the contest, Pharaoh would not listen. The spiritual insight of the magicians was greater than that of the king. So the God of Moses and Aaron continued to demonstrate with further "plagues" his superior power over the gods of the Egyptians.

After the Israelites had left Egypt and were on their way to the promised land of Canaan, God revealed his Law to them. First he gave them the Ten Commandments. The best-known of these must surely be the first and second commandments (Exodus 20:3-6), which prohibit the worship of other gods... implying that there indeed ARE other gods – gods with a small "g". The initial command: "You shall have no other gods before me" was immediately expanded to prohibit making and worshiping images or idols. It is true that the idols themselves are only wood, stone, etc., but they are nevertheless significant. For example, in Exodus 32, note the strong reactions of God and Moses when the Israelites made and worshiped the golden bull-calf. Paul, in 1 Corinthians 10:19-20, insists that offerings made to pagan idols are actually offerings to the demons associated with the idols, and are therefore absolutely forbidden to Christians. Breaking this commandment resulted in punishment which affected not only the guilty parties themselves, but also their descendants for several generations. Deuteronomy 28 lists in great detail the blessings resulting from obedience to God's Law. It also warns of the curses which are brought on by disobedience.

The third commandment tells us: "Thou shalt not take the name of the Lord thy God in vain," (Exodus 20:7, KJV). This important commandment is frequently trivialized. The traditional English translation is often taken to mean merely that we should not use God's name in thoughtless blasphemy. However, I believe that Today's English Version of the Bible reveals another dimension of what was on God's heart when it translates this commandment: "Do not use my name for evil purposes." I suspect that this means that we are prohibited from trying to use the power of the name of God Almighty to bring about or achieve things which are not in line with his will. This must also be extended to include how we use the power of the name of Jesus.

Many other prohibitions of the law of God are conveniently summarized in Deuteronomy 18:9-13. These things were practiced by the nations which surrounded Israel at that time. Indeed, the three practices on which I will focus – divination and the use of omens, spells and charms, and necromancy (attempting to communicate with dead people) – are still today found world-wide and are permitted within most of the world's religious systems.

Because the practice of these things on the part of God's people represents a lack of faith in the Lord and a trust in other spiritual powers, the passage in Deuteronomy closes with a call to be totally faithful to the Lord.

The first "disgusting practice" is found in verse 10: "Don't let your people practice divination or look for omens." Both of these are methods of foretelling the future. While it is wise to consider the future and make plans and preparations for it, it is wrong to try to find out exactly what will happen in the coming days and years. The people of Israel, often following the example of their kings, constantly sinned in this way. They reaped the consequences which God had spelled out to them in the Law. We can read of their failures in these matters in such passages as 2 Kings 17:17, 1 Chronicles 10:13-14, 2 Chronicles 33:6 and Ezekiel 13:17-23.

Deuteronomy 18:9-13 goes on to forbid the use of "spells or charms." These are used in an attempt to control what happens in the future. Whether they are things we do or objects we possess, they represent attempts to make the future go the way we want.....good fortune for ourselves perhaps, or ill-fortune for others. All such attempts are forbidden.

The third prohibition tells us, "And don't let them consult the spirits of the dead." This practice is regarded by God as especially evil. There are many passages in the scriptures where it is strictly forbidden, such as Leviticus 20:6,27. Death was to be the penalty for mediums or spiritists, and God warned that he would cut off from his people any who consulted them. King Saul, after having quite rightly forbidden mediums and fortune-tellers earlier in his reign, finally consulted one (1 Samuel 28). This action cost him his life.

God's covenant with his people made it clear the Israelites were to worship him only. They were not to pay respect to any other god. But even while God was giving his laws and talking to Moses on Mount Sinai, the Israelites, worried that their leader would not return, urged Aaron to make a golden calf (Exodus 32). It seems that as soon as they became anxious, they wanted a visible god like the nations around them.

Joshua, the Israelites' next leader, was aware that everyone *will* worship some god or spirit being. The question was really which god would the people choose to worship? He placed this choice clearly before the people in Joshua 24:15: "If you are not willing to serve him (i.e. the Lord), decide today whom you will serve, the gods your ancestors worshiped in Mesopotamia or the gods of the Amorites, in whose land you are now living."

Even though the people told Joshua they would worship the Lord, when they settled in the promised land they constantly gave way to the temptation to worship the local gods. Although they had been given strict instructions to destroy every vestige of the pagan religions around them, they failed to do so. They did not continue to worship the Lord alone. They turned to local gods, the baalim and asherim. They thought that these gods would have the experience and power to give fertility to their crops and animals, so it was these gods that they consulted about day-to-day matters. This situation went on for generation after generation, despite protests from the prophets.

In the familiar story of David and Goliath in 1 Samuel 17, we see the conflict between the Israelites and the Philistines on three levels. There are two armies conducting psychological warfare against each other. There are two champions coming face to face. But the real conflict is at another level. We are told that Goliath called down curses from his god on David. David answered: "This very day the LORD will put you in my power." David, Goliath and their armies saw it as a battle between their gods, just as Elijah did on Mount Carmel in 1 Kings 17. (Today, in some [sun dar] Kung Fu fighting, the conflict is seen as a contest between the spirits indwelling the combatants.) The Philistine army fled because the test-case had gone against them. David's God had defeated the Philistine god. The Israelites pursued and killed many of the Philistines in further skirmishes. This is our position today. The key battle has already been fought. Jesus has defeated Satan on the cross. We are still involved in skirmishes with the defeated enemy.

In the Old Testament, there are a number of other references to evil spirits. These are not apparent in some English versions, where unhelpful translations such as "satyr" or "hairy goat" are used. For instance Lev. 17:7, Psalm 91:5, Psalm 121:6, and Isa. 34:14 refer to demons.

We can see ample evidence of conflict between the Lord and evil spirits in the Old Testament. We shall find yet more spiritual conflict as we look briefly at the New Testament.

As we read of Jesus' ministry, it is immediately obvious that his presence disturbed evil spirits. He stirred them up and he was able to cast them out. Healing diseases and casting out demons were two of the main characteristics of Jesus' ministry. He also commissioned his disciples: "Jesus...gave them power and authority to drive out all demons and to cure diseases," (Luke 9:1).

The Gospel accounts distinguish between Jesus healing diseases and casting out demons. One such passage is found in Mark 1:32,34: "... people brought to Jesus all the sick and those who had demons.....Jesus healed many who were sick with all kinds of diseases and drove out many demons." In the Greek, a person troubled by evil spirits is described as being under the influence or power of a demon, never as "possessed." The action of Jesus, and later that of his disciples, was to drive the evil spirit or demon out.

Mark 1:23-27 describes a man with an evil spirit who came into the synagogue. The spirit knew who Jesus was even though the teachers of the Jews did not recognize him. Jesus told the spirit to be quiet. Today this action is commonly called "binding the spirit." Then he ordered the spirit to come out. At this, there was a violent reaction and noise, but the evil spirit came out and left.

The most detailed account of Jesus dealing with evil spirits is in Mark 5:1-20, and in the parallel passages in Luke 8:26-39 and Matthew 8:28-34. The man in this passage had several clear signs of the presence of demons:

–It was recognized by people around that the man was demonized (verse 2).
–The man had tremendous strength, more than anyone could cope with. . . . superhuman strength (verse 4).
–He suffered from uncontrolled rage (verse 4).
–He was in a state of confusion. Although he came running to Jesus for help, he was afraid of him (verses 6-7).
–The man knew who Jesus was, although he had not been told. This was psychic or clairvoyant knowledge (verse 7).
–There may have been a change of voice. Mark 1:12 tells us "the spirits begged Jesus. . ." It is probable that when the demons spoke, they were recognized by the change of voice.

Some of these characteristics can also occur in some psychiatric illnesses, but opposition to Jesus is a distinctive mark in those who are troubled by evil spirits. Nowadays, opposition to the Holy Spirit or to Christian people who are filled with the Holy Spirit may also be a sign of demonization. It is interesting to note, as Kurt Koch has pointed out, that evil spirits are disturbed in this way only by Christian people or the Bible, and by no one and nothing else. Those who are affected by evil spirits often find it very difficult even to say the name of Jesus when the spirits are active in them.

We can see from the scriptures that there is a distinct difference between the way Jesus dealt with sickness and how he handled evil spirits. When he was faced with a sick person, he often touched the person. When confronted by someone who was demonized, Jesus spoke to the demon, but did not touch the person.

There are one or two instances which might seem like exceptions to this principle, but in these cases, either it is unclear which was happening, or both sickness and demons were present together. The exact wording of the story of the epileptic boy suggests that he had *both* a physical illness *and* a demon. Luke, himself a physician, says in Luke 9:42 that Jesus commanded or rebuked (Greek: "epitimaō") the spirit, a word which is also used elsewhere in relation to the expulsion of demons. He immediately goes on to say that Jesus healed the boy, using a word (Greek: "iasis") which he uses in other places for physical healing.

Matthew, recording the same event (17:18), uses the Greek word "therapeuō" to describe Jesus' healing of the boy. This Greek word is the one most commonly used to describe physical healing. Mark (9:26-27) says, "The spirit screamed, threw the boy into a bad fit, and came out. The boy looked like a corpse, and everyone said, 'He is dead!' But Jesus took the boy by the hand and helped him to rise, and he stood up." So, although Mark does not use a word for physical healing, his reference to Jesus taking the boy by the hand after commanding the demon to leave is consistent with healing as a second stage.

The account of a woman crippled by a spirit in Luke 13:10-13 is briefer, and we have only the one account. However, it is reasonable to suggest a similar sequence of events, i.e. that Jesus placed his hand on the woman for physical healing after he had driven out the evil spirit. Long term demonization (18 years in this case) can produce physical symptoms which require separate prayer for healing to correct a change which has taken place in the body (here, prolonged stooping).

Matthew 12:43-45 and Luke 11:24-26 record an interesting story Jesus told about an evil spirit returning to a person after it had left. Jesus told this story after being accused of casting out demons by the power of Beelzebul (Satan). He responded to the accusation by saying that no one can break into a strong man's house and take away his belongings unless he first ties up the strong man. Then he can plunder his house. The "house" is a person who is infested by a demon, or "strong man," but Jesus both claims and demonstrates that he is stronger. He can break into the house and plunder it, driving out the demons.

Jesus continues, talking about an evil spirit which simply "goes out" of a person. In my opinion Jesus is not talking here about an evil spirit which he has driven out by his authority, as in the case of a strong man being overcome by a stronger one. If that had happened, the "house" would be immediately refilled and occupied by the Holy Spirit. It seems likely that Jesus is referring here to the case of a person who is *not* a believer who has a demon. This evil spirit then leaves, perhaps through other spirit powers (driven out by Beelzebul), but when it decides to return, there is no other occupant of the "house." The practical implications of this story, i.e. how to prevent the return of demons, will be discussed later.

When we look further into the New Testament, we find that the Apostles and other preachers had the same kind of encounters with evil spirits as Jesus had. In fact, from Acts 8:5-7, we can infer that these demons were not only disturbed, but cast out at the time of the individual's conversion. This, it seems to me, is what we should be aiming for.

A more detailed account of a spirit's response is found in Acts 16:16-18. A slave girl had a spirit which enabled her to predict the future. This girl recognized Paul and his companions by means of the spirit's power, and she followed them around, calling out, "These men are servants of the Most High God! They announce to you how you can be saved!" It is not clear why Paul resisted this free publicity. Perhaps he found it a distraction from what he was trying to say. Whatever the reason, Paul simply ordered the spirit to leave in the name of Jesus Christ, and it left. This is an example of someone who had only the beginning of faith being delivered from demonic power.

Acts 19 records several interesting encounters between Paul and the forces of darkness. It starts with Paul teaching, baptizing, and then laying hands on a group of believers to receive the Holy Spirit. They began to speak in tongues and prophesy. After this, Paul spent much time discussing and persuading men in the synagogue about the kingdom of God, as well as demonstrating the power of God. Unusual miracles were happening as Paul spent his time proclaiming God's message. Items which Paul had used were taken to sick and demonized people, "and their diseases were driven away, and the evil spirits would go out of them," (v.12). The words and works of Paul went hand in hand. The words explain the works, and the works prove the truth of the words. This is a general feature throughout the scriptures.

Because they had seen Paul performing unusual miracles, some Jews decided to copy his technique. Unfortunately for them, they did not have spiritual authority; they were relying only on a formula. This situation can easily arise today.

It seems to me that people who act like this are in danger of breaking the third commandment.

The seven sons of Sceva thought they could simply copy Paul's technique. When they tried it, the evil spirit knew that they did not have the authority of Jesus and his servant, Paul. The man with the evil spirit attacked them so violently that they were overcome.

It is interesting to note that, at this point, the Greek word "exorkizō" (the source of the English word "exorcize") is used. This is the only place in the Bible where this Greek word is used in this sense. It is usually used to mean "to appeal" or "to adjure." The Bible normally uses a word meaning "to cast out" rather than "to exorcize." But in the case of the sons of Sceva, "exorcize" seems to be an appropriate word to use, since it refers to attempts to drive out evil spirits by magical means, or by the use of a formula.

This demonstration of the devastating effect of evil spirits, and of the mighty power of Jesus Christ to defeat them, led many of the believers to confess openly their dealings with evil spirits. Many of them brought out their books on magic and burned them publicly. The estimated value of these books in today's terms came to around US$1,300,000 or HK$10,000,000.

Unbelievers reacted very differently to these demonstrations of the power of Jesus. The Ephesians made money from the worship of Artemis, and stood to lose a great deal if their goddess were discredited. So Demetrius, a silversmith, incited a riot in an attempt to prevent loss of trade. If we substituted the name of almost any city in Southeast Asia for the name Ephesus beginning in Acts 19:23, and changed the name Artemis to, for instance, Kuan Yin, we could imagine it all happening today.

Satan chooses his strategies to correspond to the weaknesses of his victims, whether those victims are individuals or whole culture-groups. For several centuries he has been almost completely successful in persuading educated people in the West that he does not exist. (The uneducated have not been so easily deceived.) In much of Asia, Africa, and South America, he has persuaded most of the population that his demonic representatives are "strong men" who must be served, or at least be bribed, but cannot be resisted.

Both views are dangerously false, being based on Satan's deceits. The next chapter deals with ways in which Satan may have tricked us into serving or at least acknowledging him. The final chapter describes how we can free ourselves (and others) from any claim that he may have on us.

INTO THE LIGHT

We are each affected by the culture in which we grow up without realizing it. Often cultures contain *occult** elements, of which even Christians can be totally unaware. This is true of both East and West. We will take a look at some of the distinctively Chinese forms which this occultism can take.

Although occultism can be found world-wide, there are particular local styles and variations. In Chinese culture we might call this "folk-religion" or "traditional Chinese religion." This is not the same as the structured religious system of Buddhism or Taoism which we read about in textbooks of comparative religion.

When anyone with a Chinese cultural background wishes to become a Christian, it is useful to check several points relating to his previous religious culture, so that all unhelpful influences can be put behind him. People who fully deal with these areas at the beginning of their Christian lives make more rapid growth as Christians. Indeed, experience leads me to believe that much non-growth or slow growth in young Christians is because they have not been freed from every influence of their non-Christian religion. For these people, the struggle to live

---

*Occult: dark, hidden, magic. Used here to refer to the realm of darkness, the dominion of Satan.

their Christian life is rather like trying to get out of a swamp, or to crawl out from under a tent which has collapsed.

This section deals with things which may have happened in an individual's pre-Christian days and which can cause problems later in his Christian life. I will ask each question directly, so that either you can use it yourself as a spiritual check-list, or you can use the questions in counseling those who are not growing as Christians. If you have done any of these things *since* you became a Christian, they are probably having a severe effect on your growth as a Christian and may even be causing you to lose your faith.

The first word of the gospel is "repent," and if there has been sin against the first command-ment, that is the place for repentance to begin.

Worship of Other Gods

In the Ten Commandments, the very first commandment states that we are to worship ONLY God, the creator of heaven and earth. The New Testament extends this to Jesus Christ, God's Son, and the Holy Spirit whom they have sent. So the first point to check is:

Have you, at any time, worshiped any other god, spirit, person or thing?

This worship may have taken place in a temple or in front of an idol shelf in your own home. It may well have been simply something you did as a child because you were following family practices. If this was the case, although you were not fully responsible for what you did, you could still be suffering from the effects of it.

Common ways of worshiping in the Chinese culture include burning joss sticks or making offerings of fruit or other things. Asking any god or spirit for help is also a form of worship. It is common practice in some industries, such as building or film-making, to worship spirit gods at the start of each project.

The question of ancestors poses a problem. What is done in front of photographs or tablets of dead ancestors might, in some families, be considered worship; in other families, the same action could be seen simply as respect; it depends on the way your particular family thinks. However, you yourself need to consider what was in your mind when you performed those actions. Was your attitude one of rightful respect and reverence, or was it wrong worship? How would your family members interpret your participation in such activities in the future? As a Christian, you will need to consider these questions in deciding what your involvement will be.

Did you consider that your ancestors were more important and had more power after their deaths than when they were alive? Have you done anything in front of their pictures or tablets, or at their graves, which you would not have done in front of them when they were alive (for instance, kneeling, bowing down, or burning joss sticks)? If your answer to either question is "Yes," then you should probably regard it as worship.

Were you, as a baby or child, ever offered to a spirit god?

Many small children are offered to Kuan Yin (pronounced "gwan yin" in Mandarin, "goon yum" in Cantonese, and commonly referred to in English as the "goddess of mercy"). Some are offered to other gods. This is a practice which can be found world-wide.

If you were ever offered to a spirit god it can have a powerful influence on you, until the action is repudiated in the name of Jesus.

For example, one lady had been struggling in her spiritual life for several years. She did not know that she had been offered to Kuan Yin until, during a time of ministry, the spirit within her spoke out: "Her mother asked me to look after her. I've been here a long time, and I'm staying." There was a spiritual battle for some minutes, but eventually the spirit had to give way to the name of Jesus! As a result, she had a deeper awareness of Jesus in her life and closer fellowship with his people.

If you know you were offered to a spirit god, you should try to find out whether any record of it was made at the temple, in a book, or possibly on the temple wall. If it was recorded, make every effort to have the entry erased.

When you were ill, have you ever sought healing from spirit powers? Or, more likely, did your parents ever try to get you healed by spirit power when you were ill as a child?

You may have been taken to the temple while ill and some sort of ritual may have been performed over you. Alternatively, your clothes might have been taken to the temple and "processed". (Because I am never quite sure whether to call such an action "blessing" or "cursing," I use the neutral term "processing.") This usually involves the clothes being stamped to show that the "processing" has been carried out, and then they are brought home for the child to wear.

Another common practice to obtain healing is to get a piece of paper from the temple, usually yellow or red with characters (i.e. a charm) written on it. The paper is taken home, burnt, and the ashes are added to some water which is then drunk by the invalid.

I was once praying with a young lady who had previously received healing by spirit power. After I had prayed for her, I asked her how she felt. "I feel like I want to strip my clothes off," she replied! I paused, somewhat embarrassed. She went on to explain that in the past her clothes had been taken to the temple to be "processed." "I feel that I am wearing those clothes, and they seem filthy to me now!" I prayed that God would reclothe her in the white garments which are the righteousness of Christ. This was most likely a word of wisdom, for she went away happy, no longer feeling the need to strip off her clothes!

Dr. Kurt Koch, who has world-wide experience of counseling those who have been involved with occult activity, sums up the effect of such practices as these with the words: "Every person healed through the influence of mediumistic forces suffers a death-like blow to his faith. He falls victim to a kind of spiritualistic ban."* When physical healing occurs through spirit powers, the spirits will certainly use the influence they have gained to exercise some control over that person's life.

---

*Occult Bondage and Deliverance, Kurt Koch, Grand Rapids, Mi., 1979.

Reading the Future by
Spirit Power

Have you ever attempted to learn about your future? Or has anyone ever done so on your behalf?

A great variety of methods are used all around the world for reading the future. They are used by all classes of people, and even by those who deny belief in either God or the supernatural.

I have a friend in Hong Kong who works for an engineering company and he says that whenever a fortune-teller visits the offices, there is always a long queue of those who want to have their fortunes told. Nearly all his colleagues join the queue, many of them university graduates.

Some of the methods of fortune-telling popular among Chinese people are:

–Going to the temple. A variety of methods for telling the future may be used there. A common one involves shaking a container of marked sticks, noting which ones fall out, and then having them interpreted by a professional fortune-teller.
–Consulting the basket-god, the coin-god, or using a pendulum which swings over the sand to draw a Chinese character.
–Reading the stars, tea-leaves, hands, facial features, etc.

–Visiting amateur or professional fortune-tellers who read the future by consulting a spirit guide. They usually go into a trance to do this.

–*Fung shui.* This literally means "wind-water," and its technical name is geomancy. It concerns the correct orientation for a new building, and even the correct orientation of furniture and fittings in an individual's house or business. Many people take this very seriously. The practitioner may be using occult powers.

A major Chinese bank engaged an architect to design a new main branch building in a large city in Asia. When the building was almost completed, someone realized that the architect had not consulted a fung-shui expert. So the management hurriedly brought in a fung-shui man from Hong Kong. After studying the way the building had been planned, the expert concluded that there would be a strong flow of some spiritual substance right through the building. He said this was a very serious matter, because the flow would carry away all the bank's profits. Fortunately this man was able to suggest an alternative to pulling the bank down, and rebuilding it on a different site with a different orientation. He told the management that if a particular type of tree were planted in front of the bank, it would split the flow of this spirit river and divert it around the bank. Then there would be no problem. I cannot guarantee the truth of the fung-shui part of this story, but I have seen the tree outside that particular bank.

As fung-shui has developed, it has incorporated accurate observations and elements of common sense. For example, there is an obvious practical benefit in avoiding the placement of windows and doors on the north side of buildings in China, where the north wind is bitterly cold. This is quite apart from any claimed "spirit" benefit. As with other such activities, the important question is: What is in the mind of the person doing it? Is he trusting in (or fearing) some spirit power?

Here are two examples which illustrate the sort of thing that can happen as a result of people consulting fortune-tellers:

Chi Keung was a young man of twenty who had been a Christian for some years. He began to realize that his habit of flirting with all the girls he met was wrong. (I myself had noticed that he was very aware of the opposite sex.) He confessed this failing to God, but it still kept on happening.

While he was working with me as a team member in "Life in the Spirit" seminars, I pointed out during the teaching that it was important to deal with any past occult involvement.

The Holy Spirit brought back to his memory that when he was about 10 years old, in Hong Kong, his father had taken him to an astrologer to have his horoscope cast. The astrologer had predicted that girls would find him very attractive and that he would have many girl friends. So Chi Keung confessed the sin of going to the astrologer and renounced any link with him. During the following weeks, he found that the temptation to flirt with girls had gone, and so had bad dreams which had been troubling him. This incident happened quite a long time ago, and I can add that he has now been happily married for a number of years.

The second example concerns a young lady called Lai Chun. As a group of us were talking one evening, prior to praying together, Lai Chun told us that she feared having an accident in the street. Some years before, a fortune teller had told her that she would be knocked down and killed in a street accident. She had prayed for peace of mind and tried to be unconcerned, but the fear kept returning.

When we divided up into groups for prayer, I joined the group that Lai Chun was in. I prayed for protection, then asked her to renounce her dealing with the fortune teller. When she had done that, I prayed, "cutting her off" from the fortune teller, i.e. breaking any spiritual link between them.

About six weeks later, Lai Chun told us that she had recently been in the main street in Birmingham, watching someone else on the road. Not noticing that the traffic lights had just changed, she stepped out onto the road. A car braked only just in time to avoid knocking her down. (My heart sank, because it sounded as though the fortune teller's words were near to being fulfilled.)

As she ran to the island in the center of the road, she thought, "I must be more careful next time" instead of, "It's no good trying to do anything–it's bound to happen one day." At that point, she knew that the curse had in fact been broken!

These and similar examples lead me to conclude that fortune tellers whose predictions *do* come to pass are not really looking into the future. They make it seem as if the future is fixed, and that they are merely speaking out that which is bound to happen. But what they are really doing is cursing their "customers" and then telling them what that curse is. It is the working out of this curse which shows the power of the fortune teller. Any such prediction should therefore be treated as a curse and be broken in the name of Jesus. We must be consistent and do this *even if the prediction is of something pleasant*, of good fortune, of prosperity. If something which appears good comes as a result of a fortune teller's words, there will always be a heavy price to pay in another area of life, probably mental or spiritual. This is similar to the healing by spirit power I have already mentioned.

Spells (Curses) and Charms

If, at any time, you have put a curse on someone else, you need to repent and break the curse. It is possible that you have put a curse on someone without really intending to do so. If, as a father, I were to say with real determination to my child, "You will never be any good!" I may in fact be cursing him in such a way that he never will be any good. This is especially true if the same words are repeated with conviction. Phrases like "I wish you were dead" or "I hate you," if said with sufficient conviction, or if they are said repeatedly, can also put a curse on people. (We may even put a curse on ourselves with a strong, "I wish I were dead" or similar phrase.)

You may have gone to the temple to pray against someone and may have used some sort of ritual or incantation; or maybe you have been helped by a temple keeper, priest, witch, bomoh, shaman or similar person. If this is the case, then you have used spiritistic powers and have probably put a curse into operation. If you have done any of these things, you certainly need to repent, and if you consider that the intention behind what you did amounted to a curse, you need to break the curse.

All around the world there are minor variations on the theme of "good luck." Many people keep certain things which they think will bring them good fortune, or will protect them. Such objects are referred to as charms, talismans or amulets.

Other people go through special rituals to try to keep themselves safe and to make life go well. It is, of course, right for us as Christians to pray for our safety and protection; that is simply putting our trust in God, the Father of our Lord Jesus Christ. But if our trust is in anything else, then it is wrong. Many English footballers, for example, have "lucky mascots" which they take with them to their matches. Some of them go through little rituals or routines before going out of the dressing room onto the playing field. Clearly, the object of itself does not give protection (or prosperity, etc.). They are trusting in some power which is linked to the object without even realizing it. They are putting their trust in something other than God himself. If any benefit comes from these actions at all, then that benefit must come from some spirit power which is not from God.

Because so many people keep or wear things which are meant to bring good luck, whenever someone comes to me for counseling I always look to see if the person concerned is wearing anything around his or her neck. If I can see a fine gold chain or leather thong which goes underneath his or her clothing, I am very interested to know what is on the end of it. Often it is a quite harmless object. Sometimes it is a cross or crucifix...in which case I wonder whether the individual's trust is in the object which he is wearing, or in the Person whom it represents. If the object has some non-Christian significance, then I ask the person to remove it while we are talking. Later, I will discuss the possibility of destroying it.

A Chinese university professor was counseling a man who appeared to be deeply troubled, and was making no progress in the conversation. The professor noticed a ring the man was wearing. Because he thought it looked evil, he asked the man to remove the ring. As soon as it was off, the man fell onto the floor and began to writhe about in torment. The professor was then able to drive out a number of spirits. The man later explained that the ring had been given to him when he had visited a monastery in Tibet.

Do you have in your possession anything in which anyone trusts to bring good fortune?

It could be anything of non-Christian religious significance, in which either you yourself or others might trust. This includes not only objects, but also words. It is common to have words which are intended to bring good fortune, or "blessing," which may have been written in a temple. They are usually written on red or yellow paper, and sometimes they are sealed in (often triangular) packets so that the exact contents are not known to the owner.

Putting one's trust in *things* rather than in the living God, is sinful. But quite apart from it being sinful, such paper packets and other similar objects can have an effect simply by their presence in a place.

A young Chinese lady, who was a nurse, had become a Christian. She was given wise guidance from those who were caring for her spiritually, and she destroyed several charms which had been in her possession. However, her friends still felt that there was something "dark" about her room. They also noticed that she did not seem to be making good progress in her Christian life. Eventually, she wondered if there might be a paper charm which she had missed. Although she had already glanced at the books on her bookshelf to see if there was anything between the pages, she now went through them in earnest, page by page. At last she found a piece of red paper with a Chinese "blessing" on it. After she had destroyed it, the room no longer seemed dark and she began to make progress in her Christian life.

**

Mei Ling was a Christian who had already had several experiences with the forces of darkness, including being freed from a curse, which I shall describe later. So, on this occasion, she was able to recognize that it was something of that sort which was causing her trouble. She called several Christian friends to pray with her. At one point during prayer she was rolling about on the floor, but by the time her friends left, she was feeling better. A few days before this, a friend who had recently come from Asia had left a little packet wrapped in brown paper with Mei Ling. It was to be passed on to a friend, so Mei Ling left the packet on a shelf. She thought nothing more about it until the friend came to collect it. The friend opened the packet in Mei Ling's presence. She then saw that it was an object with evil spirit significance. It became obvious that it had been the presence of this "charm," in its brown paper wrapping on her shelf, which had caused her problems.

Perhaps, as you have been reading this, you have been reminded of an object in your possession. You have maybe thought: "It's nothing, really, just something my grandmother gave me. I've kept it just in case it does bring good luck, but I don't really believe in it." If such thoughts come to your mind, it is probably best to be safe and destroy the object in question. As these last two examples show, such objects can affect people who do not even know of their presence. Ignorance is no protection.

In general, my guidelines are that anything with non-Christian symbols or form should be destroyed. So also should anything that has probably been used in non-Christian worship, or prayed over in a non-Christian setting. Small figures which have the pupils of their eyes carved in are very suspect, because spirit power is often invoked into them at the point at which their eyes are "opened." Charms, and all types of objects with demonic association, have considerable power to prevent or hinder spiritual growth. People can be severely hindered spiritually by the possession of charms and by past dealings with spirit influences.

Mary had become a Christian, but she had a charm which she was unwilling to destroy at that time. Although she had Christian friends who were caring for her spiritually, she grew very little during the next fourteen months, and was very restricted by the effects of her former habits and customs. Eventually Mary told a friend that she was now willing to destroy several things, so we agreed to meet with her. She brought a red packet, a small pendant-type Buddha from Thailand, and a pot "laughing Buddha" which looked mass-produced. She confessed her previous involvement with fortune tellers, of going to the temple, of burning joss-sticks, of going to seances, and of being healed by spirit healers. I cut her off from all these influences. Then she burnt the packet. She did not know what it contained but it was probably a charm-text. Finally she broke the charms with a hammer. She tried to persuade me to break them for her but I insisted that she, as the owner, should be the one to destroy them.

After this, I prayed reclaiming any part of her personality that had been affected and asking for her to be filled with the Holy Spirit. I also prayed to close the psychic door and to clothe her in the spiritual armor described in Ephesians 6:13-18.

A few days later Mary came up to me and embraced me, saying joyfully, "Now I am free!" Over the next few months we saw steady growth in her spiritual vitality.

This experience caused me to wonder whether it had been right to lead Mary to the Lord before she was willing to let go of her links with evil spirit worship. When a person first becomes a Christian, should he immediately repent of all known violations of the first commandment, as well as repenting generally? I think he should repent of major violations of which he is aware, but it may not be practicable to make a thorough check at the time of commitment. However, careful enquiry should be made during follow-up teaching or baptismal preparation.

There can be considerable uncertainty about what should be destroyed, and what need not be. For instance, jade, even if it has no particular shape, has occult significance to many Chinese but would have no such significance to a Western person. Some symbols and designs may have an evil meaning in one culture, but no particular meaning or significance in another. Generally young Christians, because they have been aware of a struggle with evil forces, are prepared to destroy anything, even if it has monetary value, rather than take risks.

If an object or picture has not been "processed" in a temple, but has clear non-Christian symbolism, then it is, in effect, "advertizing" the enemy. I am told of a lady who was reluctant to destroy such a thing until a friend said, "How would your husband feel if you had the picture of another man on your bedside table?" She destroyed the article!

In some parts of Asia there has been discussion about the need to destroy anything which carries a dragon symbol. I am telling the following story to illustrate that God can guide His people through such dilemmas, and can then confirm their actions, rather than to say that every dragon symbol must be destroyed.

While visiting a small Christian community, I learned that they had been encountering a number of difficulties during the previous weeks. Since there was a great deal of spirit worship in the neighboring village, I suggested that we should pray through the buildings and the grounds. One of the areas we prayed over had probably once been used as a shrine. In another place, there were three small trees growing in three clay pots with dragon designs on them. The leader of the community was uncertain what to do, but eventually decided she would take no chances. One morning she transplanted the trees from the pots, prayed over the pots and then destroyed them.

That same afternoon several members of the community were out for a walk in the village, when a lady offered them some plants. The plants were in three clay pots exactly the same as the previous ones, but without the dragons. In this way, God confirmed to the members of the community that they had done the right thing when they destroyed the pots with dragon decorations by immediately supplying them with dragon-free replacements.

Attempted Communication with the Dead: Seances or Necromancy

Have you ever attempted to communicate with a dead person?

All over the world and in every age, people have attempted to get in touch with the dead. Those who have recently been bereaved are especially open to the temptation of trying to find out whether their loved ones are at peace or not.

This is done everywhere in much the same way. A person (referred to as a *medium, channeler,* or a *sensitive* in the West, and a *shaman, witch doctor, bomoh,* etc. in the East) goes into a trance. He or she then allows him/herself to be controlled by a spirit guide, and begins to receive messages which appear to come from the dead person. The medium speaks in a voice which, generally, is different from his own (i.e. in the voice of the controlling spirit), and the message may include information which is not known to any human being except the bereaved person and the one who has died. For example, the medium might mention intimate pet-names a couple used between themselves, but which were not known to any other person.

Such a display of private information can be very convincing. However, if we are aware that there are spirit beings around, we can suppose that they are able to listen to intimate conversations. They, therefore, can have the necessary information. Their spy network is evidently enormous, and these spirits are quick to use the information they have gathered as a form of spiritual blackmail.

Controlling spirits, acting through a medium, will often claim to offer information about the future and to heal sickness. The comments made above about fortune-tellers and faith healers apply here as well.

A single visit to a medium, even if it is only as an observer, can blunt a person's spiritual growth. Repentance and renunciation are essential if spiritual progress is to be restored. If there is any hint that you yourself have mediumistic powers, you should renounce them.

If any relatives, alive or dead, have mediumistic powers, it is important to break the spiritistic links between yourself and them. Dr. Kurt Koch has pointed out that when someone with mediumistic powers dies, these powers will pass on to someone else. The medium may choose this person, so that in effect, he bequeaths his powers to a successor. But if this is not consciously done, the powers are likely to pass down the family line.

So, if a Christian becomes aware of "spiritual darkness" around him, but does not know of any sin which might have caused it, it is worth asking whether any relative has died recently...it could be that he has received an unwelcome inheritance.

By "spiritual darkness" I mean a reduced sense of the light of God's presence. Such a person may also experience a reduced sense of closeness to God in prayer, "dryness" in Bible reading, and the loss of desire for Christian fellowship and worship.

Such spiritual darkness may also be caused by some relative or close friend praying for the person in a temple or in front of a spirit shelf. I have known of cases where Chinese students in England have become aware of "spiritual darkness." A few days later, they have received letters from home saying that someone, probably their mother, has been praying to Kuan Yin or some other god for their success in forthcoming examinations. What was intended for their welfare has brought them spiritual difficulty because dark forces were being focused on Christians.

Victims of the Environment

Up to now, we have been considering mostly situations in which you may have been suffering difficulty as a result of sins you have committed. However, the Bible makes it clear that we are not isolated individuals; we are affected by the world around us. When we enjoy good things such as nice food, fresh water, safe homes, literature, music, leisure activities, and a reasonably safe and just environment, we benefit from the good work of other people. But sometimes we suffer because of the sin and selfishness of others. Similarly, we experience blessings and curses through the good deeds and misdeeds of those around us, especially of our family and ancestors. People can be adversely affected by curses from members of their family.

Mei Ling was going through a period of depression. She did not think it was anything of a spiritual nature. Perhaps it was a word of knowledge which caused me to feel that it was wrong for this child of God to be ill, but whatever the reason, I was prompted to make some enquiries. Two of Mei Ling's relatives had died recently, so I decided to investigate further.

For some weeks Mei Ling's hands had felt cold, both to her and to anyone who touched them. She had a headache and depression. Five years previously, while at school, she had had severe depression. She had been so ill that she had been sent to Taiwan for Western-type medical investigation. The doctors had found no psychiatric or physical cause for her illness. They had said the sickness must be hereditary in origin. During this present episode, she had again been for medical help and had seen a counselor, but no one had been able to help her.

I asked about the two dead relatives. Mei Ling had happy memories of one, but was not greatly grieved. She had not liked the other at all. Strangely, this dead relative had appeared to her several times since her death. I asked whether the relative had had any dealings with the occult. Mei Ling said that she used to go to mediums, like everyone else, but she did not think that the woman had been a medium herself. Her mother had told her that the relative was "good with charms."

We now had a possible explanation for Mei Ling's present trouble: depression linked with the dead relative. But what about the similarity with the previous depression? I asked Mei Ling if she had had any contact with that particular relative at the time she was depressed previously. Was there any antagonism between her and the rest of the family?

Mei Ling's face slowly lit up as she remembered. The woman's daughter had married Mei Ling's cousin, but the cousin had deserted his wife at the time a baby was due. This had made the relative very angry with the family. Mei Ling also remembered that her mother had wanted to take her to a medium because she thought Mei Ling was under a curse. She had asked Mei Ling whether an image of the woman had appeared to her, explaining that, if someone is cursed he often "sees" the person who has put the curse on him.

So, both periods of depression and illness had a link with the same relative who was known to have an interest in spirit powers. I thought we had the explanation – Mei Ling was sure we had! Now we used the authority given to us by Jesus to break the curse. I claimed protection for us and for anyone around, then I asked Mei Ling to cut herself off from all psychic influence from her father and his line, from her mother and her line, and from this relative. I felt it was not necessary to name the relative, but to identify her as "the person who lives at..." She did as I suggested, and I confirmed it, reclaiming any area of her personality which had been affected. I closed the psychic door, and prayed for her to be filled and blessed with the Holy Spirit.

While we were praying, the image of the relative came to Mei Ling again, then shrank and melted away like smoke from a chimney. The headache disappeared immediately, and her friend reported the next day that she was better. When I checked with her about three months later, Mei Ling reported no further trouble with depression or headaches. She was surprised that I had asked.

Mei Ling's story illustrates a general principle: when a person or a family experiences more than their share of misfortunes, it is wise to consider the possibility of a curse on the individual or family. This is especially important when these misfortunes are unconnected, when they do not have any clear explanation, or in the case of illness, when there is no clear medical diagnosis. Obviously individuals and families are liable to misfortune simply because of the fallen world in which we live. It is when the number of such happenings is excessive that we should look for a curse.

Some typical misfortunes might be:
- –unconnected sicknesses
- –breakdown of family relationships
- –being excessively prone to accidents
- –suicidal tendencies
- –repeated miscarriages and related female problems
- –break-downs of cars, household appliances, etc.
- –mental or emotional breakdown
- –sense of frustration and pessimism, even when circumstances are not particularly difficult
- –continuing financial problems even though the income seems sufficient

Ah Fong had been experiencing severe gastric troubles. She had been to the student health service and had been examined, but there had been no real diagnosis. She had once taken an overdose of acetomenophen. She suffered from fear, inferiority, curiosity and low self-esteem. In a dream or perhaps when she was half awake, she had felt herself under attack, and had resisted in the name of Jesus. She had heard voices telling her that she would do better in her studies if she did not go to church. Sometimes, when she had been reading the Bible, the words she read were completely opposite to those actually on the printed page. For example, instead of seeing "God is love," she would read "God is not love."

Ah Fong told us that she had often visited temples with her mother, who spent much time there. She also told us her brother suffered depression and undiagnosed mental illness.

Although a friend and I prayed with Ah Fong, broke any psychic bondages to her family, and commanded any spirits to name themselves, there was no response. Neither of us was satisfied; we did not feel that the matter had been cleared up.

A few days later Ah Fong remembered something her mother had told her when she was about ten years old. When her mother was carrying her, a man named Chi Sahn had put the family under a curse. The curse was intended to make Ah Fong's mother hate her husband, although he is a gentle and loving man. The curse was brought into effect by giving her mother and 3 year-old brother "processed" fruit to eat.

When Ah Fong's grandfather heard of this, he sent a potion, which her mother took. Drinking the potion freed her from the curse of hating her husband (but I suspect it might have put her under some other bondage). As this was after Ah Fong was born, she herself was not freed from the original curse, nor was her brother.

Her Christian friend took action immediately. He claimed protection, took authority, broke the curse and cut her free from Chi Sahn. There was a visible reaction. After a few more minutes of prayer, Ah Fong said that she was filled with peace. An x-ray a few days later showed nothing amiss, and she had no further intestinal trouble.

In the two examples above, the curse was the result of the direct action of an individual against a family. In some cases, however, it is not possible to identify the origin of the curse. It may arise from a general or specific breaking of the first and second commandments by ancestors. Or it might be the commandment to honor one's father and mother which has been broken by the person or by his ancestors. This is, however, much less common in Chinese society than in Western, because of the great importance of 'filial piety' among the Chinese. On the other hand, the tight family ties among Chinese may cause the individual to be more subject to the effects of the sins of his ancestors than in the West.

Certainly, many disturbing effects pass down a Chinese family, and it may be difficult to tell the difference between those which are specifically of a spiritual nature and those which arise from natural family characteristics and upbringing. The powerful effects of a close family environment can easily be overlooked.

The following story is an example of a spirit (rather than a curse) which followed several generations of a family, but where the origin was completely unknown.

A strong Christian, Mrs. Fung was making a significant contribution to her local church, as well as counseling people from nearby towns. However, she often felt a little guilty and wondered if she was doing as much as she should for the Lord.

Her mentally confused father-in-law had lived with the Fungs for eighteen months. She had watched his personality go to pieces and she had wondered if she could have done more to help him. He had died as recently as the previous week.

When she thought about her family, she had a sense of heaviness, unbelief, and undefined guilt. She felt trapped. Her sense of depression became apparent when she began to speak in tongues.

As we moved into prayer, her prayer betrayed a sense of effort and of undefined guilt. The phrase "accuser of the brethren" came into my mind, followed a moment later by "accusing spirit." I hesitated, because this lady had been counseled many times before, and I did not think she could have a spirit. However, I claimed protection, bound any evil spirit present, and told it, in the name of Jesus, to go. She started spluttering and looked as if she was coughing. So I began commanding with confidence and authority. Before I had finished, it had gone.

Mrs. Fung told me that, on previous occasions, she had been delivered from other spirits, but this one had been the fiercest. She said it had been curled up inside her at the bottom of her back. As she continued talking, she realized that this **was** in fact the heaviness which she had sensed over the family and over herself.

She could now recognize it in the family for two generations back, and it was already apparent in her twenty year-old daughter, who showed the same self-accusation.

Later she said, "It's marvellous! The accusing voice is silent for the first time in years!" I meet Mrs. Fung from time to time, and so I know that the effect has been permanent.

It seems that evil influences can work through places as well as through people. Some people who visit temples, even as tourists and not as worshipers, can find themselves affected badly. People have often asked me to pray with them concerning such visits, when they have begun to realize that they were affected. This has been particularly true of the Snake Temple in Penang. I would advise people to avoid visiting temples without some very specific reason. Whenever I am walking past a temple myself, I pray quietly, asking Jesus to protect me, and continue in tongues. Once, as I was walking along a side street in Singapore, I became aware of a darkness, and started to pray as an automatic reaction. A few moments later I saw an Indian temple set back behind the houses. I had become aware of its spiritual darkness before I had seen it.

The next story shows how a person can be affected by the things going on in and around the place where he lives.

Mei Ying had been a Christian for about a year when it came to light that she had been involved in many occult activities in the past. We had several sessions together in which she was very co-operative in repenting of her past actions and renouncing the consequences. We also needed to deal with several evil spirits. But her depression and spiritual weakness seemed to linger on, whatever we did.

At the time, Mei Ying was living in a student hostel. We learned that the girl in the room next to her, and also the girl across the corridor, were worshiping Kuan Yin daily. We decided that Mei Ying was not spiritually strong enough to resist the resulting evil pressure, so we arranged for her to move out of the student hostel. The improvement in her condition was rapid and permanent.

When people become Christians while they are still living in a place where spirit worship is taking place, they need a great deal of spiritual support. They need to bind the spiritual forces around them and to claim protection night and morning, as I will explain in the next chapter.

From time to time, buildings may need to be cleansed. I would advise any Christian, when moving into a new house, or even into an hotel bedroom, to pray in it before sleeping there. But even if this is done on first arrival, it may need to be repeated. Here is an exceptional example of spirit power in a house.

Some years ago I visited a large town in northern England with the pastor and two members of the Birmingham Chinese Christian Fellowship. Our aim was to see if the time was right to start a Chinese Christian Fellowship there. When we reached the home where we were to stay for several days, our friends showed us an article from the local newspaper of the previous day. Here are some extracts from it:

> Police were today called in to investigate a case which it was believed might involve "evil spirits" influencing a local Chinese restaurant family. Five members of the family were taken to hospital but were found to have nothing medically wrong with them. One of the sons said: "Everything's a mess and mixed up.

"Things began to happen after my grand-mother died in China two weeks ago. There is a possibility that my family could be influenced by the idea of evil spirits, but we are Christians and don't believe in them. Last Saturday a relative visited us, but she collapsed and was taken to hospital. Earlier that day, my brother had fallen down the stairs and he, too, needed hospital treatment." He went on to say that the past week or so had been a series of misfortunes, but events came to a head at 5 a.m. today when his brother again collapsed on the landing of their home. He said that "somebody" woke him up and told him to follow. When he got to the landing, "it" pushed him down the stairs. He continued: "Another brother of mine is still suffering from a fever and at about 5.30 a.m. I heard my third brother moaning. He was alright when he went to bed, but we just could not wake him up, and he was taken unconscious to hospital."

Doctors at the hospital found nothing medically wrong with any of them. To add to their troubles, their family doctor has asked for their names to be removed from his list. Police checked the possibility of a gas leak, but the Gas Board discovered none. The town's Medical Officer of Health said an inspector had visited the home and was satisfied that the incident had nothing to do with public health matters. (Sunderland Echo, 16-3-74, P.2, and 18-3-74, P.10, used by permission.)

We knew nothing about this family until we read this item in the newspaper. We went round to see them, and found that the mother had been praying that a Chinese pastor would visit them, although she did not know of any Chinese pastor in England. We talked with them and the next day we prayed through the house. There has been no further trouble. Neither the medical authorities nor the public health inspector had been able to solve the mystery; but it had been cleared up in the name of Jesus!

I was intrigued by the attitude of the family; they thought that because they were Christians, and did not believe in such things as evil spirits, that their troubles could not have been caused by spirits. Unfortunately, evil spirits are not courteous enough to leave alone those who do not believe in them!

There are other activities which are likely to cause trouble, and should be renounced in the same way as spiritistic activities. These include:

–KUNG FU and other MARTIAL ARTS. This is particularly important when there has been an initiation ceremony and when evil spirits have been deliberately invited into the body to reduce pain and increase strength, as in *sun dar* ("spirit boxing"). All forms of Kung Fu in which there is an actual or implied opponent (or partner) should be treated with suspicion, as should any ritual which is not an essential part of the exercise.

An instructor may have occult influence on his students even though the physical movements he is teaching are harmless in themselves.

Ming Chai, who had been a Christian for a number of years, had great difficulty in controlling his temper. Sometimes he would go round and round his room, beating his fists violently against the wall, before he could bring his temper under control. Years before, he had done some Kung Fu. He had not done a great deal, but nevertheless, he now decided he should renounce it, and he did so.

A few days later at work, a friend was talking to him, and, in order to make a point, he put his hands to Ming Chai's throat. Ming Chai quietly allowed himself to be pushed back against the wall. He realized that previously in such a situation, he would have reacted spontaneously with an uncontrollable Kung Fu movement. Time showed that his temper problem had been completely solved.

–TRANSCENDENTAL MEDITATION. This (and similar activities) is a means of opening up the personality. The methods used are generally similar to traditional Christian meditation, but are different in one vital way... they are not done in the name of Jesus, nor under the protection of the Holy Spirit. If you have used a mantra (a mantra is a word which is repeated many times as a form of prayer), then you certainly need to repent. In transcendental meditation, the mantra is the name of a Hindu god. However, this is generally not explained to the person being initiated. The correct Christian alternative would be to use the name of Jesus.

–SECRET SOCIETIES. Membership of a secret society, such as a Triad gang or a Masonic Lodge, needs to be repented of. Here again, any secret words or names must be renounced. If you were given the words under oath of secrecy, you may need friends to help you to break completely free. Speaking the name or words in the presence of other Christians is often sufficient to break their power.

BECOMING FREE

It is possible that as you have been reading the last chapter, you have remembered that you have had some involvement with one or more of the activities which I have been describing. It may have been long ago, and you may have only been a child at the time. Or you might feel that you are subject to a curse. In either case, you may be able to free yourself from the effects on your own, by prayer. This may be satisfactory if the effect of your past activities, or of the curse, seems to be only slight, or if it is something which has come to light after you have already received ministry from someone else. However, I feel that it is generally best to go for help to Christians who have experience in these areas.

Up to this point, I have been writing as though I were speaking directly to the person who needs help, but from here on, I shall be writing as if addressing the person who is giving that help.

The activities described in the previous chapter are all likely to lead to trouble and should be checked carefully. Any objects which have been used in these activities, such as charms, talismans, "magic" writing on paper and so on, should be destroyed. Books related to occult activities, including story books, need to be destroyed too. Generally, it is helpful at the same time to deal with any books and magazines which clearly teach a non-Christian religion or philosophy, or are pornographic. [I am not saying that it is never right for a Christian to possess books about the occult, or non-Christian religions. Such books could be useful to a well-established Christian, especially if his ministry involves helping people who hold to these religions and ideas. However, books which have anti-Christian material may be dangerous for young Christians.]

When a group of Christians gathers to help a person, the meeting can probably proceed as follows:

a) Someone should pray that God will, through the power of the Holy Spirit, protect everyone present, and also all their relatives and others who are close to them. It is helpful to sing one or two worship songs.

b) The person who needs help should reaffirm his or her faith in Jesus Christ, and then pray a prayer of confession and repentance. The form of prayer could be something like this: "Jesus is my Lord and my God. Lord God, Father of Jesus Christ, I confess to you as sinful every dealing with forces opposed to Jesus, which I or my ancestors have been involved in. In particular, I confess _____ (speaker confesses his specific known sins.) I repent of my sins and, with your help, will not repeat them." (The need to include confession of the sins of ancestors is indicated by such passages as Exodus 20:5, Leviticus 26:39-40, Nehemiah 1:6, and Jeremiah 32:18.)

c) At this point, it is very helpful for the leader to thank God for the forgiveness that is available in Jesus and to assure the repentant person that he or she is truly forgiven. Among some groups this is known as absolution. The person being helped may now be encouraged to pray, thanking the Lord for his forgiveness.

This procedure is sufficient for most sins. However, when the sin has involved some sort of deliberate dealing with Satan, it is important that another step be taken. This particular step is called renunciation.

Let me illustrate. Some years ago, I was working in the Research and Development department of a large engineering company. Our chief metallurgist needed to visit Russia to discuss a new development in welding technology. In the same department was a very skilled technical librarian who had been born in Latvia (part of the USSR) and had spent her childhood there. Since she spoke fluent Russian and also had a general understanding of the technology involved, she seemed to be an ideal person to go with the chief metallurgist as his interpreter. When she applied to go, the British Foreign Office refused to give her permission. The reason was very interesting. She had acquired British nationality by marrying a British citizen and the Foreign Office could therefore look after her interests in any country of the world.... except in Russia. As well as being a British citizen, she was also still a Russian citizen. If she returned to Russia she would be totally under the control of the Russian authorities. In that situation, the British Consul could do nothing to help her. When she became a British citizen, she could have renounced her Russian citizenship but she had not chosen to do so. So she would still be under Russian authority when in Russian territory.

If in the past we have had any dealings with the enemy, it seems that in some way he retains a claim on us, just as though we were one of his citizens. This situation will continue until we specifically and deliberately renounce that connection. A prayer of renunciation could be worded something like this:

> I now renounce everything opposed to Jesus, which may have influenced me in any way. I renounce Satan and all his deceitful works. In the Name of Jesus I break any curse that may have come upon me and I claim freedom from all the powers of darkness. Jesus is my Lord!

Where the details are known (for example, about any person or circumstance which may have imposed a curse) these should be added in to the prayer at this point.

If the person being prayed for has ever been initiated into a secret society (e.g. a Triad or a Masonic Lodge) or witches' coven, he needs to specifically renounce all the promises he made and any new name which he was given at the time.

If any member of the person's family is (or has been) a fortune-teller, a medium, or particularly involved in temple worship, then any family or psychic link with that person should also be renounced and broken in the name of Jesus.

d) At this point, the leader also should take authority in the name of Jesus and add weight to what has already been done. He should break any curse and break any claim which the enemy might have on the person being helped; he should bind any spirits which are present and order them to show themselves briefly and then to depart.

e) When I am ministering, I then continue with several other prayers which I believe will consolidate what has been done. I pray, reclaiming for Jesus any area of the personality which has been affected by Satan. I then ask the Holy Spirit to flow into that area and to restore it to what Jesus would want it to be. I go on to ask the Holy Spirit to repair any part of the person's spiritual defences which may have been weakened by the things they have done, or by the misdeeds of their ancestors or other people. This process is sometimes referred to as "closing the psychic door."

If there is any suggestion that the person has been healed from sickness by spirit power, repentance and breaking of any resulting curse is essential. Another stage is also necessary. When the power of the original (evil spirit) healing is broken and renounced, the sickness may come back, immediately or after a period of time. So we also pray asking *Jesus* to heal the old sickness to prevent it reappearing.

It is important that any objects which need to be destroyed are destroyed *by the owner.* To destroy the offending objects, anything that can be burned should be burned. The remains should be prayed over and put in the rubbish bin. If the object cannot be burned, it should be broken. If it cannot be broken, it should at least be bent with a hammer or a heavy stone. Occasionally the person who is being helped will have a charm or something of the sort, which belongs to someone else in his family, and he may feel that he has no right to destroy it. In this case, he should return it to someone who is responsible for it, perhaps the head of the family, or Granny.

I am convinced that anyone who wishes to become a Christian should be questioned about all his previous dealings with satanic forces. If repentance at the time of conversion is to be truly meaningful, then it must include repentance of every act in which the first and second commandments were broken. In practice, it may not be possible to go through every incident at the time of conversion. However, all areas of such satanic involvement should be checked through as soon as possible.

I have observed that water baptism can set a seal on this cleaning-up process. On several occasions, we have ministered to new Christians as incidents from their non-Christian past came back to their memory. This ministry continued over a period of weeks, but as soon as the converts were baptized in water, their problems ceased immediately.

It is a long-standing tradition in the church to ask three questions before baptism. They are generally worded something like this:

1) Do you renounce the devil and all his works?

2) Do you acknowledge Jesus Christ as your Savior, your Lord and your God?

3) Do you intend to serve Him in the fellowship of His people?

Unfortunately, in some churches the first of these questions has been either dropped or changed. I believe the first question is important, especially for people who have come out of a spiritistic background. Once people from such backgrounds have renounced the devil and all his works, they frequently make very rapid progress in their Christian faith because they are so accustomed to dealing with the spiritual realm.

Always check to make sure a person is free from satanic or occult links before praying for the Holy Spirit to come in power. If the Holy Spirit comes powerfully into someone and encounters spiritual darkness, there may be a good deal of disturbance, including mental disturbance.

It is sometimes difficult to know how best to help children when their parents become Christians. If they are ten or twelve years old and if they are able to understand such things, they can be guided through a prayer time similar to adults.

This is especially desirable if they have themselves repented and come to a personal faith in Jesus. Everything should be kept as simple and low-key as possible to avoid frightening them. Indeed, they may already be frightened but they will be reassured by learning of the power of Christ. One young lady, after witnessing a rather spectacular deliverance from Kung Fu spirits in Birmingham, told me that she had been terrified of evil spirits ("ghosts") as a child in Hong Kong. "Why didn't our Sunday School teachers tell us that they were subject to us in the name of Jesus?!" she asked. Even small children can be taught to use the name of Jesus for their own protection.

Parents of small children can minister to them by praying over them in their sleep. I suggest that this is a valuable thing for all Christian parents to do in any case. The prayer can be for specific matters concerning the child or can be prayer in tongues. Parents have a right to pray in this way, but only for children who have not yet reached the age when they are responsible for themselves. An older person is in control of his own decisions. It would be wrong and ineffective to try to make important decisions for him. The parents of one young child prayed for him, while he slept, to be freed from an evil spirit. The next morning he described what had seemed to him to be a dream, in which something nasty and black jumped out of him and ran away.

After this initial cleaning-up process, it is important that the person concerned remains clean.

He must be especially careful not to go into any situation which would bring him into temptation. He should also avoid situations where there is worship of evil forces, such as temples. His defences against satanic powers will become stronger as he engages in the normal activities of the Christian life – reading the Bible, prayer, taking communion, meeting for fellowship with other Christians, worship and so on.

It is important that he should particularly pray for protection from all the forces of darkness as he settles down to sleep at night, and when he first wakes up in the morning. It seems that the period between waking and sleeping is a time when our defences are lowered. Many times people have told me they have had a sense of being attacked when they were in a state of drowsiness. It can take the form of oppression, of becoming aware of darkness, or even of physical pressure on the chest or throat.

If at these or any other times a Christian senses he is being attacked by some evil force, he should immediately call out something like, "Evil spirit, I bind you in the name of Jesus and tell you to go from me!" If he has any idea of the name of the spirit (e.g. lust), then it can be addressed by that name. It may be necessary to repeat the command two or three times.

The best advice that can be given to anyone who has repented of his sins with satanic forces is that which Jesus gave to the woman who was caught in adultery in John 8:11 – "Go, but do not sin again."

Deliverance

Up to now, I have been considering situations in which evil forces have been pressing onto a person and have led him or her into sin. There are, however, times when those evil forces have actually gained some sort of entry into someone's personality. This condition has been described by psychiatrists as "the possession syndrome."*

I would want to limit the use of the word "possession" to those cases in which satanic forces are in full control. I believe that, even in such cases, the "possessed" person still has sufficient freedom of will to be able to choose between evil forces and Jesus. The battle may, of course, be a very hard one. This condition is rare and I do not believe a Christian can be possessed. However, it is relatively common for someone's personality to have been infiltrated by an evil spirit, and a Christian can certainly be affected.

In order to understand more clearly what is really happening when demonic forces gain entry to a person's life, it is helpful to think of a rat or lizard which gets into my house or flat. The intruder could cause some damage. It might even frighten me. But the house or flat still belongs to me and the rat has no right to be here. To get rid of the unwanted visitor, I can invite friends to join me in

---

*For example, see Dr. Yap's account of his observations in Hong Kong in *Journal of Mental Science*, Vol 106, No. 114, Jan 1960.

driving it out. Evil spirits, just like rats, are relatively common and many people around us do need help in ejecting them. Like rats, they can be vicious, so we need to exercise care when we are dealing with them. It is well known that rats are attracted to garbage. If there is garbage left around, it will be more difficult to keep the rats out. Similarly, if there continues to be unconfessed sin in my life, it will be more difficult to keep the demons away.

Whenever we are going through the cleaning-up process which I have been describing, we need to be prepared for spirits to show themselves.

When I first met Tai Ming, he was a student. He had been a Christian about two months. He had been brought up in traditional Chinese religion and was the oldest child in his family. When he was around sixteen, he felt ignored by his family and he became very determined and strong-willed. Tai Ming had investigated several other religions, but came to regard both Buddhism and Hinduism as inadequate.

One day, while writing a self-assessment, he began questioning himself. He realized that he had no purpose in life and that he felt very inadequate. So he had decided to go downstairs and talk to some Christians who lived there. As a result, Tai Ming became a Christian himself. He began to change; he became less sarcastic and less prone to losing his temper, so he felt he was making progress in the Christian life.

Suddenly something occurred which caused him to go down spiritually. When I saw him, he did not feel able to tell me what the problem was, but he did tell me that one day, while in a group praying, he felt a strong desire to "see something evil." It had taken six people to hold him in his chair! A few days later at college, he had wanted to vomit. He was obviously very disturbed and since then, everything had seemed to go wrong.

When he got to this point in telling his story, because there were only four of us altogether, I decided to send for reinforcements...it looked as if we could need greater prayer strength to combat the enemy (and just possibly physical strength).

Tai Ming went on with his story. He had often burned incense both in the home and the temple and had prayed to gods, especially to Kuan Yin. When he was thirteen years old, he had had skin trouble for which doctors could do nothing. It was cured in the temple.

While he was still at school, his parents went to a medium to find out what results he was going to get in an examination. He had experimented with ESP (extra sensory perception) and had twice seen a spirit. Both his grandmother and his uncle's wife frequently consulted mediums.

Since it was then exam time, I asked him whether it was likely that members of his family would have been praying in the temple for him to do well on his exams. (Such prayer, although offered with good intentions, can have a negative effect on Christians, presumably because it brings them to the enemy's attention.) He thought it was quite probable. I suggested that it could have been his family's prayers which may have started off his present problems. Although the idea came as a surprise to him, he readily accepted it.

I went on to ask him if he felt able to forgive the people who might have been involved in such praying. He replied that he could forgive two of them but he was having problems forgiving the third. He said he would ask God to help him forgive.

Because an English pastor had previously prayed with him, and had taken him through confession about burning joss sticks, Tai Ming was familiar with the process of confession. However, before we started praying, I gave him a plastic bag in case he felt like vomiting. Even the mention of it made him feel like it.

I then went on to ask Tai Ming to tell Jesus that he was sorry for all his past involvements with evil forces, in as much detail as he could remember. I asked him to promise Jesus that he would not do such things again. This he did, whereupon he vomited a little. I then pronounced forgiveness, broke any curses and cut him off from any evil spiritual connections with his family.

At this point, the spirit began to manifest itself. He began to bounce in his chair until it fell over backwards. Then he began to crawl around the floor. As he was doing this, I bound the spirit, telling it not to harm or tear him. He then took up a peculiar position on the floor, which some-one later identified with the monkey god.

I asked him to look into my eyes but he did not respond. He told me later that he could not do it. Since we did not know the name of the spirit, I just ordered it to go, and the whole group of us sang praises as Tai Ming continued to move around the floor. After about ten minutes, there was a change. I asked him if the spirit had gone. "I think so," he replied. We got him back into the chair. He was exhausted.

I asked him to say "Jesus is Lord, Jesus is my Lord," and "I belong to Jesus," which he did, although in a weak whisper. He said he felt clear, but his heart was beating rapidly and he was all churned up inside. I decided to pray, asking that the Holy Spirit anoint him and bring him inner peace. Then, as there was no resistance from him, I reclaim-ed for Jesus any areas which Satan had affected.

He was still shaky, but now able to talk, and he thanked us repeatedly. He said he had wanted to punch me in the nose, but had not been able to!

I advised him to claim protection night and morning. About six weeks later I heard that Tai Ming was behaving normally. When I visited the town where he was studying four months later, he told me that he is now perfectly alright.

Sometimes we can be reasonably certain that spirits are present in someone, because they have specifically invited them in. For example someone might have asked for strength for Kung Fu fighting ("sun dar"). If this has happened, the repentance and renunciation which I have detailed in the previous section should be followed by a deliverance session which I am about to describe.

Sometimes it is not clear if spirits are present. It might be helpful to check through the following list of indications of demonization:

a) A compulsion to sin which the person is unable to overcome, although he has made serious attempts at self-discipline. This can include strong addictions, such as to alcohol, narcotics, sexual perversion and so on. However, as with other items in this list, compulsion alone would not be a certain indication of the presence of evil spirits. Deep inner healing might be called for rather than deliverance.

b) Violent aggressive behavior and exceptional strength as in "running amok," the Malay version of demonization.

c) Unrest and possibly anger in the presence of Christians and in Christian worship; even tearing a Bible. Afterwards, a person who has been acting in such ways may say, "I don't know why I did it. I couldn't stop myself."

d) Difficulty in saying the name of Jesus, especially in a prayerful context.

e) Uncontrollable blasphemy.

f) Continuously being gripped by fear, even when there is no danger of any sort.

g) Paranormal knowledge and healing abilities, as observed in 19th century China by J.L. Nevius in *Demon Possession and Allied Themes*, and continuing widely today.

Most of these phenomena could occur without any demon being present at all. Indeed, there seems to be a tendency in some quarters today to blame demons for every difficulty and weakness of the will, and to start shouting at them. I consider this unwise. If the person being prayed with realizes that no spirit has gone, he may think: "This wise and experienced Christian who is helping me discerned a spirit, but it has not gone. So it is still in me. I am demonized! How terrible! And as it did not go when this gifted person prayed with me, it is going to dominate me for the rest of my life."

On the other hand, if the person thinks a spirit has gone when it hasn't because it was not there, he may think: "Now all my troubles are ended!" and may fail to nurture his discipleship with prayer and make every effort to resist temptation.

There are times when, although there are definite indications of demonization, we cannot be sure. I then explain very carefully that I am going to command any spirit that may be present, but if nothing happens it very probably means that there was no spirit in the first place. In that case, I shall suggest other methods of dealing with the particular problem, methods which encourage discipleship development and spiritual growth.

It is important to realize that here I am mainly considering spirits which have a link with a particular sin or with occult activities. Evil spirits are also encountered in other circumstances, and those spirits seem to have somewhat different characteristics. They may be encountered when we are dealing with inner healing, rather than with occult involvement.

Bei Chin came from a Christian home and had been a Christian as long as she could remember. When I first met her, she was married, in her thirties, and struggling with deep depression. As we prayed, she forgave a number of people and received forgiveness. The Lord brought back forgotten memories and healed them, including a difficult birth experience. In the following weeks, her depression steadily lifted and she gradually came off medication.

As she became more alert and aware of herself, she realized that she was still troubled by insecurity, jealousy and anger. So we had another counseling session. The ministry session centered on the period of her life when she was about four years old and another baby had joined the family. We prayed about various incidents and saw the Lord continuing his healing work. This second ministry time started something more. As she yielded herself more completely to the Holy Spirit, there was increasing conflict between the Lord and an evil spirit within her. She described the inner battle as terrifying in its intensity – more intense than anything she had ever experienced. Her anger over little frustrations was boundless. She knew Satan was very active, but also knew that the name of Jesus brought peace. Something had to be done.

The third ministry session was quite brief. The violent spirit was expelled from Bei Chin in Jesus name, and she knew immediately that her healing was complete. Afterwards, she knew peace as she had never known it before. She wrote to me saying, "I believe that I needed to have everything else sorted out first during the two previous ministry sessions. I have thought about the way someone described it – the stone was removed and the beetle emerged. Well, now it's gone and I praise the Lord."

It seems that if demons are to stay in a person, they need to have somewhere to hide, something to put their roots into. Most commonly, this is sin with the occult. But it may be other sins, such as sins against the body: drug or alcohol addiction, wrongful sexual activity and so forth. And in addition, it seems that evil spirits can hide in *emotional wounds*. Before effective deliverance can take place, whatever sin is involved must be cleansed through repentance and forgiveness and *any deep emotional wound must be healed.* Otherwise, there is a serious probability that the demon will return.

In the course of prayer for inner healing, as in the example described above, we may dislodge unsuspected demons. These demons are sometimes called "personality spirits" as their names are often personality traits such as fear, anger or jealousy. When they show themselves, they are dealt with in the same way as other evil spirits. I doubt if there is any fundamental difference between demons hooked into occult sin and those hooked into emotional wounds. The latter sometimes seem to be rather less vicious but are equally harmful and evil.

Personally, I never like to undertake counseling unless I have at least one other person with me. If deliverance is likely, I prefer to have a team of no less than four people, of whom two or three have some experience in that area. The team can include one person as a "trainee." If the person who is being helped has been deeply involved in occult activities, then it is good to have a small group somewhere else backing us up in prayer at the same time.

The deliverance session should generally include the following sections:

a) We should always start with prayer for protection, asking God, by the power of the Holy Spirit, to watch over us and guard us. We should also pray that He will protect our families (naming those close to us) and others connected with us.

b) Before getting into the actual deliverance, it is wise to ask the person who needs help to repent of any relevant sins. Indeed, he or she should repent of all known sins. This should be done in the way previously described in the "cleaning-up" section. Then the person should state clearly that he wants Jesus to be Lord of his life.

This is especially important as a preliminary to deliverance. I have been told that sometimes during an attempted deliverance, the spirit has replied to the counselor's command to leave, "I'm not going, because he wants me to stay!" I should not like this to happen to me! Jesus will not deliver a person against his will. So it is important for me to know, and for the person to clearly state, that he wants the spirit to leave. Then I can reply to the spirit, "He does *not* want you. Jesus is Lord of all his life."

c) Now the person who is being helped should renounce the spirit and order it out himself. He or she should tell it to go to the place to which Jesus would send it. It is important to emphasize that this needs to be a definite order and not a prayer. I believe that some attempts at deliverance are not effective because people ask God or Jesus to drive out the spirit. Although there may be occasions when this is right, God has given His people clear authority over spirits, and he expects us to use that authority. It is a general principle that God will not do for us things which we can do for ourselves.

d) Unless it is quite obvious that the demon has gone, the leader should repeat the command. The general form of this order to the spirit could be something like this:

> I take authority in the name of Jesus Christ. I bind you spirit of...(whatever the spirit may be). I forbid you to cause any noise or disturbance. I forbid you to harm any person. I command you to show yourself briefly and then to go directly to the place to which Jesus would send you.

There is no need to shout. I have no reason to think that evil spirits are deaf. They do, however, seem to be of rather low intelligence and it may be necessary to repeat the command a few times. There is often a delay while they are pulling up their roots, or packing up...or whatever the correct description of their actions might be! During this time-lag, those present can pray in tongues and the command can be repeated from time to time. If there has been a thorough repentance, the grip of the spirits may have been weakened sufficiently for them to go immediately. However, a delay of from five to fifteen minutes is nothing unusual. During this time, the spirits may compel the person to make actions corresponding to their nature, as in the example of the monkey god spirit. There seems to me to be no reason for interfering with this process, unless it is likely that someone may be harmed.

It is probably sensible to avoid touching the person being delivered, unless there is an extreme emergency. Jesus laid His hands on the sick but not on the demonized.

Sometimes this stage can be speeded up by getting the person who is being delivered to look directly into the eyes of the person doing the deliverance. The ejection of demons may also be accelerated if those present sing worship songs which proclaim the Lordship of Jesus Christ.

In the suggested form of command which I gave above, I assumed that the person doing the deliverance knew the name of the demon. If this is not the case, then a phrase such as "spirit opposed to the name of Jesus" could be used instead. If there is a definite indication in the person's body or eyes that a spirit is active, the phrase used could be "spirit now showing itself." Some people, if they do not know the name of the spirit, will command it to give its name, in line with Jesus' practice in Mark 5. Although I do this sometimes, in general I regard it as a digression. We are not told that Jesus did it in connection with any of the other deliverances which he performed. It may be an unnecessary diversion, which gets us into conversation with the demon and wastes time.

Any time when deliverance may be necessary, it is wise to watch the eyes and face of the person concerned for any unusual or unexpected movements. The fingers should be watched, too. A distinctive twitching of the fingers is often the first sign that a spirit is being dislodged. Those present at a deliverance session should always keep their eyes wide open, including during the prayer time... it may be necessary to dodge!

Sometimes the spirit speaks in a voice that is noticeably different from that of the person to whom we are ministering. It may say things like "I hate you" or "Go away," even to a close friend. If this happens, it is best to either ignore it or to say, "Spirit, be quiet!" Even if such things are said in the person's usual voice, it is still best to ignore it if the things which are said are out of character. We need to realize that such negative reactions are the result of the demon speaking. The evil spirit in the demonized person hates the Holy Spirit in us.

If the spirits have been effectively dislodged by thorough repentance beforehand, when one has been ejected, the rest (if there are more) may follow in quick succession. If this is the case, the command to go should be repeated as soon as each spirit begins to show itself.

e) It is generally fairly obvious when the spirit has gone. Any agitation of the body suddenly ceases and the person relaxes. Sometimes this is more apparent to those present than it is to the person concerned.

f) What happens if the spirit does not go? It may be because there was no spirit there in the first place! As I have already pointed out, some people attempt deliverance in cases when it is not appropriate. Sometimes, when I am ministering, I am not really sure that I am dealing with a spirit at all until I see the evidence that a spirit has left.

If a spirit does not leave, it could be because the person has not really repented and renounced his sin. The demon still has a claim on him.

If it is clear that a demon is present, because of the way the person is behaving and feeling, but it has not gone in a reasonable time, it would be sensible to pause and reconsider the situation. It is unwise to continue if the team are feeling tired or if things seem to be "stuck." Equally, it is not wise to go on with such ministry if it is getting late. It is generally not helpful to continue this type of ministry for more than one or two hours, in case the team become exhausted. If spirits are continuing to show themselves after this time, then they should be bound as I am going to describe.

If the session is to be ended in such circumstances, the person doing the deliverance should forbid the spirit(s) to cause any trouble and forbid them to deceive or harm the person concerned ("binding" the spirit). Then everyone can take a break for tea! The session can either be resumed after a rest and prayer, or left until another time. If it is to be left until another time, it is probably wise to arrange for preparatory prayer, for prayer support during the forthcoming session, and possibly for a period of fasting by the person who is being helped and by some of the team who will be ministering.

Other practices which seem to help in dislodging reluctant spirits are:

–Worshiping, singing songs which exalt Jesus, and praying in tongues.
–"Breaking bread" (sharing holy communion or eucharist together).
–Reading passages of scripture such as those in the book of Revelation which speak of the downfall of the beast and which describe the glory of the returning King.

Afterwards

As the deliverance session draws to a close, it is good for all those present to worship and thank the Lord. This has the effect of consolidating what has been done. The leader will also pray (probably laying on hands and possibly anointing with oil) to reclaim for Jesus any areas of the personality which have been affected by Satan and to close any "psychic door" which may have been used as a point of entry. If that "door" was sin of some sort, it will have been dealt with already. But the sin itself may have arisen from a personality weakness or an emotional wound. For example, someone may have experienced rejection as a child and then compensated by getting into occultism or addiction, thus allowing a spirit to enter. In a situation like this there would be a real possibility of the person who had been freed from demonization going back again to his old ways if the rejection were not faced and dealt with.

A very simple matter could be discussed and prayed about at the end of the deliverance session if those present (especially the person being helped) are not too tired. But in most cases, it will be necessary to arrange for at least one more counseling session. In addition, continuing discipleship training and encouragement will probably be necessary.

Anointing with oil (for which we have a precedent in James 5:14) can serve several purposes. It can be a symbol and focus for the work of the Holy

Spirit in bringing peace to a disturbed inner being. But it can also act as an indicator of whether there is a spirit still active. Once or twice, in these circumstances, I have asked the person we were praying for, "Is it all right if, as I pray for you, I anoint you, that is touch you on the forehead with a drop of this oil?" The person, or rather the demon within, has reacted with a strong, "NO! NO!" Such a reaction would suggest that it is wise to bind the remaining spirits and plan to continue at another time.

It seems to me that, in some sense, the personality (or the memory) exists in layers, like the skins of an onion. It is possible to work on the outer layers and be satisfied that they are free of demonic interference. Then, a few months later, when the person has made progress in the Christian life, new problems show up and more deliverance is necessary. It *could* be that the old spirits have returned, but if the person has been making reasonable attempts to grow as a Christian, it is much more likely that spirits at a deeper level have been forced to reveal themselves. This can occur, even if there was no reaction to anointing.

Deliverance of Non-Christians

Deliverance, as I have described it above, is essentially the process of freeing a person who wants to become more responsive and obedient to Jesus from any evil spirit power which interferes with this desire. So the question arises as to whether it is appropriate to carry out deliverance ministry on a non-Christian.

This situation sometimes arises when a person says quite clearly that he would like to become a Christian, but he feels there is something inside him which is preventing him from making that commitment. This tension is most likely to occur if he has previously been subject to demonic influences either personally, or through his family. In such a situation, it is possible to conduct the deliverance and to lead the person to make a Christian commitment in one combined process.

It is my belief that we should be ready to do this as soon as the desire and difficulty are mentioned. I feel that there are many people around whose response to Jesus is being hindered by demonic spirits.

A friend of mine, Rev. Jimmy Song, who comes from Singapore but is now in the Anglican ministry in England, has much experience of dealing with non-Christians who need deliverance. He has people coming to him, requesting help because of enormous confusion going on deep within them. He gets referrals from a psychiatrist at a local hospital, who, when he has a patient who is making no progress, asks the patient if he has been to seances or done anything similar. When the answer is "Yes," he sends them along to my friend. This psychiatrist has discovered that Jimmy can do something with his patients that he himself can't do!

When a non-Christian comes to him, Jimmy Song will usually ask a question something like this: "Do you think Jesus Christ can help you?" If the answer is "Yes," then he considers that they have the beginnings of faith, and he goes ahead with the deliverance. Whenever he has done this, he has always been able to lead the person to Christ afterwards.

If we want to help someone, perhaps a friend or relative, who is not a Christian and may be demonized, we cannot drive out the demon until they desire deliverance, but we can bind the demon. For instance, as part of our daily devotions we might include a command something like this: "I take authority in the name of Jesus and I bind any spirit around my father which is opposed to the name of Jesus. I forbid you to make any attempt to deceive my father, or to harm him, or to interfere with the work of God being done in him." Binding prayer like this can make a marked difference in the person's response to the gospel.

Cleaning Up Places

If we pray with a person to help him get free from entanglement with evil spirits, we should also give some thought to the place where he lives, and possibly also to the place where he works. Some homes and work environments can be places where evil influences reside. It is therefore important to deal with these too, so that the person does not end up being dragged back into that from which he has been delivered.

If the person concerned is free to do what he wishes in his home, especially if he is the head of the household, the situation is quite straightforward.

1) The members of the household, together with one or two other Christians to give them encouragement and guidance, should meet in the main room of the house to pray. They should ask the Lord to protect them and their families, while they are coming against any evil spirits in the home.

2) Everything associated with spirit worship should be destroyed. If there is an idol shelf, the owner or head of the household should break it down and burn it. Everything which can be burned should be burned, and things which will not burn should be broken or dented.

3) Prayer should be said in every room of the house or flat. A suitable prayer could be something like this:

In the name of Jesus, I bind any spirit around this place which is opposed to the name of Jesus. I tell you, you have no rights in this place. It belongs to one of Jesus' people, and I command you to leave immediately and go to the place to which Jesus would send you. Be gone in the name of Jesus! And in this place I proclaim Jesus, crucified, risen, ascended and now Lord. I ask you, Holy Spirit, to cleanse this room of any evil and fill it with the light of your presence.

It is good to pray not only for the cleansing of the room in question and for the Holy Spirit to fill the place with His presence, but also to ask God's blessing on all who will use the room. Obviously, the form of blessing will vary according to the use of each particular room. For instance, in a bedroom, we might pray that the Holy Spirit will watch over those who sleep there and will give them peace and rest. In a living room, we can pray that God will bless those who come there to eat or talk.

4) When each room in the house or flat has been dealt with, those present should return to the main room. The head of the household should be allowed the opportunity to pray, offering the whole place to God, for him to use as he wishes and directs.

The procedure just described above will normally be sufficient to free the home from any evil influences. However, it could happen that some family members still have a sensation of evil, an eerie feeling, or a sense of coldness in some places in the house. This can happen even though the general spiritual temperature of the place is now warm. If necessary, the procedure can be repeated. It would be wise this time to bring in a few more Christians, and to spend some time singing worship songs in each room, especially in those rooms where there has been a sense of evil or darkness. It is also helpful to celebrate Communion (the Lord's Supper or Eucharist) in the main room of the house or flat as an additional expression of worship.

If the head of the household or the person who is in authority in the home is not supportive of the actions described above, then the cleaning-up process cannot be as thorough as we would like it to be. We obviously cannot destroy anything without the full approval of the owner, so all that can be done is to pray in the room belonging to the Christian who is being helped. Because it is the room in which the Christian lives, he or she has some authority there. In this situation, as well as praying for the cleansing of the room from all evil influences, those praying should particularly ask the Holy Spirit to guard the doors and windows, and to put a spiritual resistance on the walls, so that evil influences will not penetrate from neighbouring rooms. Concrete walls are not necessarily resistant to spirit influences!

The illustration in the previous chapter, of a young student living in a hostel, whose neighbours were regularly worshiping Kuan Yin, shows how penetrating evil influences can be. In that case, the only solution was to move the young Christian out of that particular student hostel.

Some years ago, on my first visit to Hong Kong, I was ministering to a servant-girl who lived in the large flat of her employer. Although her employers were church-goers, they had several large figures, almost life-size, of traditional Chinese gods in their home. As they were away at the time, she was able to take me and a friend into the flat. We prayed in her room, but I did not know what to do about the large figures in the main living room. Clearly, we could not damage or deface them in any way. Eventually I decided to stand in front of each figure in turn, and I bound the spirit which it represented in the name of Jesus Christ. Unfortunately, I had no further contact with the servant-girl, so I did not find out if this had been effective.

It is wise for any Christian who is moving into a new house, flat, or even hotel bedroom, to pray over the place as described in points 3 and 4 above. Even then, the effect might not be permanent.

Years ago, I prayed through the house of a friend on the day he moved in. He was anxious to have this done before he and his family slept in the house. Several years later, he was experiencing some difficulties in his home, and he asked me to join with him in praying through the house again.

This we did, and there was an immediate improvement in the domestic situation. The only explanation I can find for this is that some evil influence had entered the house through a non-Christian relative who had stayed there for several months.

Perhaps this focus on overcoming the evil influences around us has given the impression that Christians are on the defensive all the time. It is important that we should not feel such defensiveness. A Christian who is taking discipleship with Jesus seriously will find that his authority in Christ enables him to make definite inroads into Satan's kingdom.

For Kim, becoming a Christian had been a long and difficult process. Her family actively practiced traditional Chinese religion and were strongly influenced by Buddhism. At school Kim became interested in archaeology and that led to an interest in the Bible. She had taken a Bible correspondence course, but had had it sent to another address because of the strong opposition of her parents. Partly because she wanted to be free to search for spiritual reality, Kim went to England to train as a nurse. Although she met Jehovah's Witnesses and Christian Scientists, she knew this was not what she was looking for. After her three years' training, she moved to Birmingham, still searching. There, she made contact with the Chinese Christian Fellowship, and she came to Jesus Christ in repentance and faith. But her struggles did not end there; her family strongly opposed her new faith, particularly her baptism. Eventually, they gave their consent to her being baptized. As far as Kim knew, she was the first person ever in her family to become a Christian. The way of discipleship for her was far from easy throughout the next few years. However, because she had to overcome such opposition to her Christian discipleship, Kim developed considerable spiritual maturity and became a strong Christian.

After she had been a Christian for about ten years, she, her husband and two sons went to visit her parents' home in Malaysia. Her family had continued to offer gifts to the gods daily and to burn joss sticks to the household idols. During the visit, her parents had to go away for a few days, leaving Kim, her husband and sons alone in the house. Kim's parents were now fully reconciled to her being a Christian, so they did not ask her to make the daily offerings. Instead, her sister came in each day to do what was necessary. But, every day, soon after her sister left the house, the joss stick stopped burning! While the parents were there it had burned throughout the day, but as soon as the house was occupied solely by Christians, the joss stick was unable to burn!

Kim's spiritual influence is not confined to Malaysia. While nursing in England, when she was sister-in-charge of a ward, she discovered that the ward orderlies were in the habit of playing with a ouija board when they were not busy. Although Kim told them to stop it, they continued to play with it from time to time when she was away from the ward. But they always knew when Kim was back on the ward because the ouija board stopped working!

I have told Kim's story at some length, at the end of this chapter on evil spirit forces, to make a very important point. Evil spirits are dangerous and they are powerful. But they are not all-powerful. A Christian who is taking discipleship seriously, and is living wholeheartedly for Christ, can use the authority which he has, in the name of Jesus Christ, to control and overcome all the forces of the evil one.

Summary

Summary of how to help those who may be suffering from demonic oppression:

A. Points to enquire about. Have you or your family:
1. worshiped any other god, spirit, person, or thing?
2. been offered, at any time, to any other god or to any spirit?
3. been taken at any time to a temple, medium, etc., for healing?
4. tried to read the future by spirit power (perhaps with the help of fortune-tellers, mediums, coin-god, etc.)?
5. tried to control the future (including getting prosperity or protection, etc.) by spirit power? This may involve the use of charms, curses, etc.
6. trusted any thing to protect you, bring you good fortune or "good karma"?
7. attempted to communicate with any dead person?
8. had any powers or suggestion of powers as a medium, fortune-teller, etc.?
9. had a string of unconnected misfortunes which have no simple explanation?

B. Action to take

L – Leader   C – person being counseled

1. L prays for protection and binds any demon (evil spirit) which may be present.

2. C affirms his (or her) faith in Jesus and commitment to him as Lord of his life.

3. C repents of all his dealings with other gods, and of trusting in them. (These will be the things which have come to light as a result of asking the questions in A above.)

4. L assures C that he is forgiven and freed from the spiritual penalties of his misdeeds – the penalties have been suffered by Jesus in his place.

5. C renounces all of his and his family's dealings with other gods and spirits.

6. C destroys any objects or books which he possesses which have any spirit associations. (If the objects are somewhere else, then C agrees to destroy them as soon as he can.)

7. C renounces any curse or evil influence which may have come upon him through his own wrong conduct or through the conduct of any other person.

8. L reinforces what C has just done by taking authority in the name of Jesus and breaking any curse, etc. on C, and also breaking any harmful link or bondage which may exist between him and his father, mother or other relative, as may be relevant.

9. If there is any reason to think that a demon (evil spirit) is affecting C, he renounces it, tells it to leave and to go to the place to which Jesus would send it.

10. L reinforces what C has just done by taking authority in the name of Jesus, binding any demon, commanding it to show itself very briefly, and then to go to the place to which Jesus would send it.

11. L prays for the restoring work of the Holy Spirit in C.

12. C expresses thanks to God, and renews his commitment to Jesus.

SOME USEFUL BOOKS
AND BOOKLETS

I Believe in Satan's Downfall, Michael Green, Hodder and Stoughton, London, 1981

Spiritual Warfare, M. Harper, Servant Publications, Ann Arbor, U.S.A.

Filipino Spirit World, R.L. Henry, OMF Publishers, Manila, 1986

Christian Counselling and Occultism, Kurt E. Koch, Kregel Publications, Grand Rapids, U.S.A., 1973

Healing, F. MacNutt, Ave Maria Press, Notre Dame, U.S.A., 1974 or Hodder and Stoughton, London, 1989

Demon Possession, J.L. Nevius, Kregel Publications, Grand Rapids, U.S.A., 1979. (First Published by Fleming H. Revell, 1894)

Expelling Demons, Derek Prince, Derek Prince Ministries, Fort Lauderdale, U.S.A.

But Deliver Us from Evil, J. Richards, Darton Longman and Todd, London, 1974.

Deliverance from Evil Spirits, M. Scanlan and R.J. Cirner, Servant Books, Ann Arbor, U.S.A.

The Christian Answer to Ancestral Worship, Lucy Tan, Asian Beacon, Kluang, Malaysia, 1978

Climbing Higher, Lucy Tan, Asian Beacon, Kluang, Malaysia, 1981

Comfort My People, I. and S. Lim, Methodist Book Room, Singapore, 1988

* * *

Addresses for lesser known publishers:

OMF Publishers
P.O. Box 2217
Manila, Philippines

Servant Books
Box 8617
Ann Arbor, Mi. 48107
U.S.A.

Derek Prince Ministries
P.O. Box 300
Fort Lauderdale, Fl. 33302
U.S.A.

Asian Beacon
P.O. Box 109
Kluang 86007
Johor, Malaysia

Methodist Book Room
10 Mount Sophia
Singapore 0922
Republic of Singapore.

DR. JOHN ASTON is a trained scientist with a PhD in metallurgy. Through his many years of working as a metallurgist and of teaching in university, he has developed acute skills of scientific observation, study and problem-solving. In SET FREE he brings these same skills together in his approach to dealing with demonic activity. Dr. Aston has studied at London Bible College and holds a degree in theology (DipTh) from London University. In addition, his more than 20 years of involvement in the Birmingham Chinese Christian Fellowship have given him a broad knowledge of Chinese culture and religion. Dr. Aston is also a trained prayer counselor and teaches at "Wholeness Through Christ" schools in the U.K.. He has taught seminars on prayer counseling and freedom from demonic bondage in several countries in Southeast Asia. Readers will find a practical and orderly approach to what is sometimes perceived as a strange and frightening subject.